SEASIDE WALKS
ON VANCOUVER ISLAND

SEASIDE WALKS
on Vancouver Island

THEO DOMBROWSKI

RMB

Rocky Mountain Books
www.rmbooks.com

Library and Archives Canada Cataloguing in Publication

Dombrowski, Theo, 1947-, author
    Seaside walks on Vancouver Island / Theo Dombrowski.

Includes bibliographical references and index.
Issued in print and electronic formats.
ISBN 978-1-77160-013-2 (pbk.).— ISBN 978-1-77160-014-9 (html).—
ISBN 978-1-77160-015-6 (pdf)

    1. Hiking—British Columbia—Vancouver Island—Guidebooks.
2. Trails—British Columbia—Vancouver Island—Guidebooks.
3. Vancouver Island (B.C.)—Guidebooks. I. Title.

GV199.44.C22V35 2014   796.5109711'2   C2013-908271-9
                                                 C2013-908272-7

Front cover photo: Rocky Coast at Sunset © jonmullen

Printed in Canada

Rocky Mountain Books acknowledges the financial support for its publishing program from the Government of Canada through the Canada Book Fund (CBF) and the Canada Council for the Arts, and from the province of British Columbia through the British Columbia Arts Council and the Book Publishing Tax Credit.

This book was produced using FSC®-certified, acid-free paper, processed chlorine free and printed with vegetable-based inks.

Disclaimer

CONTENTS

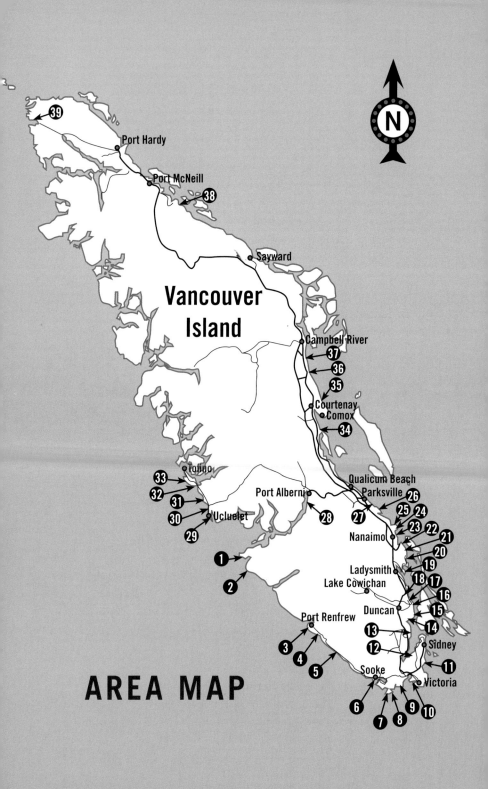

N

Port Hardy

Port McNeill

Sayward

Vancouver
Island

Campbell River

Courtenay
Comox

Tofino

Qualicum Beach
Parksville

Port Alberni

Nanaimo

Ucluelet

Ladysmith
Lake Cowichan

Duncan

Port Renfrew

Sidney

Sooke

Victoria

AREA MAP

INTRODUCTION

Vancouver Island is known worldwide for its magnificent mountains, rivers and coastline. Hikers are particularly drawn to its long-distance coastal walks – not just the world-famous West Coast Trail but also the Juan de Fuca, North Coast, Nootka, Hesquiat Peninsula and Cape Scott Trails.

It is not just backpackers who can experience the coastal wonders of the Island, however. There is a wealth of short trails, from 1 to 12 km, that bring seashore lovers to and along the shore. What they will find there is hugely varied. Quiet estuaries with sea meadows, rugged clifftop tracks exposed to the full force of the sea, and broad sandy shores with warm swimming waters – all are part of Vancouver Island's coast.

The trails in this book are selected because they are the kind of places sought out by those looking for a walk to or near the ocean. Although a few of these routes require walking along the shore in order to complete a loop, most of the emphasis is on the trails themselves rather than the shore. Still, many are described with the option of extending a walk along the shore. Not included are those (often spectacular) beaches where almost all the walking is on beaches and little on the trails approaching them. Excluded too are some very remote routes reachable only with difficult drives along active logging roads. Likewise, all of these trails except one are on Vancouver Island itself rather than the adjoining Gulf Islands. (The exception, Newcastle Island, is effectively part of Nanaimo.)

Almost all of these trails are within parks, whether administered by municipalities, regional districts, the province or the federal government. Thus, all of them are, up to a point, developed and maintained. Boardwalks, bridges and staircases are common, as are interpretive signs, outhouses and picnic tables. This is not the case, however, with all of these trails. Included are a few challenging ones, the kinds of routes that appeal to those with a zest for adventure and a taste for wilderness.

Also included, in a separate section, is exactly the opposite kind of seaside walking. In this section you will find a brief outline of the promenades, esplanades and sea walks along the harbours and waterfronts of Island towns and cities.

WEATHER

One of the great attractions of these seashore trails is that they can be enjoyed year round. In fact, many of them are particularly appealing in "off" seasons. The bright colours of autumn leaves, the storms of winter and the displays of flowers in spring make these routes attractive at any time of year.

Those visiting the trails on the west coast of the Island, though, should be prepared for the fact that the west coast receives two to three times the precipitation of the east coast. Suitable clothing and being prepared for the worst can transform a miserable experience into a pleasurable adventure.

WILDLIFE ENCOUNTERS

Vancouver Island does not have grizzlies. While it does have black bears – and many of them – they seem, mysteriously, even less likely to be aggressive than their mainland kin. Still, there have been a few exceptions. Visitors will be wise to make their presence noisily known and avoid confrontations. In fact, many of the walks in this book, especially on the west coast, are in areas where gastronomically inclined bears forage on the seashore.

Similarly, west-coast hikers bringing children along will be well advised to keep them close by. Cougar attacks on children, though rare, are more common on Vancouver Island than anywhere else in Canada.

Wolves and elk, though a concern in some places, are so elusive here as to be not worth worrying about. Vancouver Island has no porcupines, skunks, moose, coyotes, foxes, wolverines or any other potentially problematic animals.

It does, however, have seals and sea lions. It is not impossible that on some beaches you will come across a baby seal or basking sea lion. In both cases, stay well away. An apparently abandoned baby seal is almost always not, and a sleepy sea lion can become aggressively awake.

DRINKING WATER

Though locals traditionally have drunk water from fast-rushing streams, for day hikes there is no need to risk infection or even carry water purification chemicals or filters. It is best to bring tap water.

SAFETY

More than half the trails in this book are close enough to civilization that safety is no greater a concern than it would be for a walk in a local park. This is not the case, however, for all of the trails.

- The biggest danger on remote and difficult trails is probably a twisted ankle in combination with hypothermia. Walking poles, good boots, first-aid kit and proper clothing – always erring on the side of caution – are sensible insurance.

- In remote areas, the ideal group size is three or more. On easy, busy trails your judgment can obviously come into play.

- Always be prepared to turn back if weather, fitness or morale become an issue.

- Consider taking bear bells, noisemakers and/or bear spray if you are travelling in a small group in remote areas on the west coast.

- Be particularly careful on boardwalks in wet weather. They can be slippery.

- Beach logs too can be dangerously slippery when wet, not to mention unstable. Incidents of heavy beach logs rolling onto a picnicker or sunbather are far too common.

- None of the trails in this book will put you in danger of being trapped by incoming tides. However, there are a few places where, if you wander a long way down a shore on an incoming tide, you may have difficulty returning to the shore trailhead. Be alert to tidal movements. Tides tend to be high during the day in winter and out during the day in summer. A broad shore you walked easily in summer may be underwater in winter or during summer evenings.

- Never collect and eat shellfish without first checking that doing so is legal, and more important, that the Department of Fisheries has not issued a closure because of paralytic shellfish poisoning. Check www.pac.dfo-mpo.gc.ca/fm-gp/contamination/index-eng.htm or simply google the string {Canada Department Fisheries Oceans shellfish closures}.

- Rocky shores, easily walked in summer, can be dangerously slippery in other seasons.

CLOTHING AND EQUIPMENT

Much depends on the location of the trail, the time of year and the weather forecast for a particular day. As a general principle, it is better to take too many clothing options than too few. A rain jacket may add half a kilo to your pack but could prove to be invaluable. Quick-drying fabrics are ideal; avoid cotton in cold weather, including jeans. Insects can sometimes be a problem, so bring repellent and, even in hot weather, long pants (or zip-offs). Trail runners, or "approach shoes," are fine for easy trails, but ankle-height boots with a good grip can vastly improve your footing. Soft hiking boots are good enough for everything in this book – and less likely than stiffer boots to produce blisters. For two or three spectacularly muddy trails, locals sometimes wear gumboots. If you are coming during the summer and you see that a trail is easy and has extensive shorewalking, consider wearing or bringing "water shoes" – or at least shoes you won't mind getting wet as you stroll through wet patches of shore.

ACCESS

Many of these trails are in well-developed areas on the south and east coast of the Island. This means that the roads approaching them are in good condition. It also means, sometimes, that the route getting there will require a little labyrinth-managing. Usually the simplest route is given, with intermediate distances, to make life as easy as possible. A few of the most spectacular and isolated trails, however, do require driving on gravel roads. All of these are much used, (usually) well maintained and open all week.

NUMBERED TEXT

For clarity and ease of reference the trail descriptions in this book are written in short, numbered paragraphs. Some photo captions also contain numbers, which refer to the correspondingly numbered paragraphs in the text.

DIFFICULTY

These sections describe not the exertion required, but the nature of the terrain, the need for caution because of loose rock, roots, mud, slippery boardwalks and so on. While you may have to cross small streams, you will be able to use bridges over significant streams for all trails included in this book. If there is a high log bridge, it will have at least one handrail and a good walking surface.

DISTANCES

Distances are generally given as round trips. Distance figures can be misleading, however. A couple of kilometres on a steep, rough trail can seem two or three times as long as 2 km on an easy trail. This is especially true of some of the west-coast beaches like Keeha Bay and Radar Hill Beaches. Even calculating distances can be difficult, since lots of little knolls and twists can lead, in effect, to what actually is a longer trail than the distance indicated would suggest. When looking at the quoted distance in planning your hike, be sure to consider the height gain and trail difficulty information as well. In addition, don't dismiss a trail if it seems shorter than what you're looking for. Many of these routes have the option of being extended by long walks on the shore itself. Intermediate distances are provided on maps only if the trail is long enough to warrant them.

HEIGHT GAIN

This is the net difference between a route's high and low points. Many trails in this book start at their highest point and descend, sometimes steeply, toward the shore. A note is given, though, where there are many rises and falls, cumulatively making for a more strenuous walk than might otherwise seem likely. Even so, compared to many day hikes, none of the walks in this volume will be very strenuous for anyone who is reasonably fit.

SEASON

As already noted, most of these trails are actually hiked all year round. Winter and spring tend to be the muddiest times of year. Even in a rainy autumn, mud can be slow to develop. Conversely, even in a dry spring, mud can be slow to dry up.

SKETCH MAPS

Red lines indicate main trails. Red dashed lines are options. Black dashed lines are other trails, sometimes mentioned as options, but without detailed information provided.

OPTIONS TEXT

Type in light blue following a main description is used to indicate options.

1. KEEHA BEACH

A challenging, hate-it-or-love-it trek through dense, mud-prone coastal rainforest to a magically isolated stretch of exposed ocean beach.

7 km return (plan to walk additional 2–3 km on the beach)	Difficult
Starting elevation: 13 m High point: 45 m	All seasons, but August and September are best

Start: As you approach Bamfield, turn left onto South Bamfield Road and follow it a short distance. Park in a small area on the right-hand side of the road about 400 m before the trailhead (though you can drop off/pick up at the trailhead).

Difficulty: Some call this the "gumboot trail" because it has many extremely muddy sections. Be prepared to climb over fallen logs and roots. Psych yourself up to enjoy the obstacle course of a fairytale tangle of twisted trees or you may become frustrated by the slow going. Plan to take the better part of a day.

1. The first part of the trail, starting near some houses, is deceptively easy. Be prepared for wood to be slippery, however, particularly if you have Vibram soles (though waterproofs are probably the best footwear). At very high tides you will have to skirt through some trees behind a short section of shore that is normally the easier route. Before long you will come to the infamous mud, though at the end of a dry summer it can be minimal.

2. About 1.6 km along the trail (it will seem much farther), you will come to a junction with a simple sign and usually a bit of flagging tape pointing to the right to Cape Beale, some 4.5 km down this trail. (See the Options section below.)

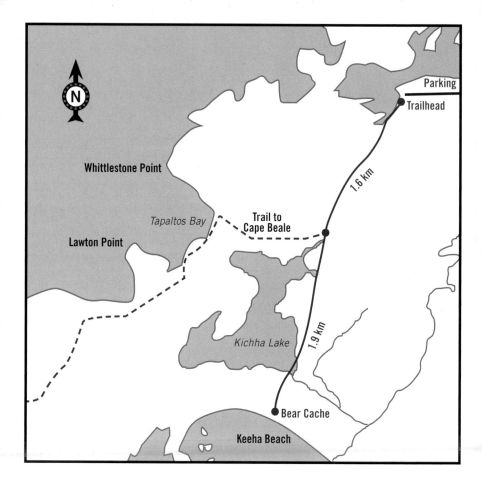

3. Soon you get your first glimpses of Kichha Lake on your right (300 m). The trail approaches the shoreline of the 1-km-long lake primarily at its southern end. Don't expect a spot suitable for picnicking or swimming, though.

4. Once you cross a boardwalk/floating bridge, the route begins a challenging ascent of the hill between you and the shore. The trail here is particularly prone to fallen logs. Once you have ascended about 30 m, the track descends; there are some ropes installed here to help when the going gets slippery. By now you will probably become aware of the roar of the surf, indicating the proximity of the beach.

ABOVE *Deer ferns, cedar, salal and hemlock fronds against one of the richly coloured patches of moss that typify the garden-like vegetation along much of the path. (1)*

BELOW *The surf can be dangerously large here, though in summer months it is usually low to moderate. (5)*

5. Only a few minutes are required to reach the beach from the bottom of the hill. Note the "bear cache," a metal structure for storing food safely for those planning to spend the night here.

6. You can explore the entire 1.7-km length of the beach. Probably the prettiest views (including a sea arch) and the best walking are along the southeast end, to your left. There is usually a small stream here, if you need water and are prepared to treat it. Look for cougar and bear tracks in the sand. Keep your eyes seaward, too, for migrating grey whales, especially in spring and fall when they come in close to the shore to feed.

7. Return by the same route.

OPTIONS

1. From the same trailhead, instead of going straight ahead at the signposted junction, turn right to hike to Tapaltos Beach along a muddy 1-km trail with scrambles over and under fallen trees. Tapaltos Bay itself is about 1 km long.

2. At the south end of Tapaltos, a few fishing buoys in the trees mark the beginning of another trail, to Cape Beale lighthouse on a rocky bluff about 50 m above crashing waves. This trail too is muddy, and more strenuous than the first section to Tapaltos Bay, rising and descending over a fairly rocky hill. You will need to balance along logs, crawl under and over deadfall and keep an eye on your route by looking for flagging tape. There is no significant beach at Cape Beale, but there are great views from the lighthouse if the tide is low enough to get out to it over a small stretch of sand. Distance from the trailhead is 6 km.

2. PACHENA POINT LIGHTHOUSE

The first stage of the world-famous West Coast Trail: deep west-coast forest, large trees, historical shipwreck sites. Good viewing spot for hundreds of sea lions on wave-swept rocks. Pachena Point lighthouse.

20 km return	Easy (but quite long)
Starting elevation: sea level High point: 110 m	All seasons (some muddy patches)

Start: From Port Alberni, follow the signs to Bamfield. After about 85 km, instead of going into Bamfield at a sharp right-hand turn, follow the sign to the West Coast Trail and arrive at the signposted parking area after 500 m.

Difficulty: This is mostly an old roadbed. It is in large part a broad, generally even surface with only gradual and moderate elevation changes. Bridges make stream crossings easy. The only challenge comes with the length. The optional side trails can involve some fairly steep scrambling.

1. Go first to the West Coast Trail office on the grassy field. While there is a quota and fee for backpackers planning to do the whole trail, there is no charge for day use. You still need to register, though, regardless.

2. Follow the wide, level trail along the edge of the hard, white sands of Pachena Beach. If the tide is low you may choose to walk along the beach and join the trail.

3. The trail crosses Clonard Creek over a little bridge and runs close to the shoreline under large firs and hemlocks for the next 2 km. It is possible to take a few side jaunts

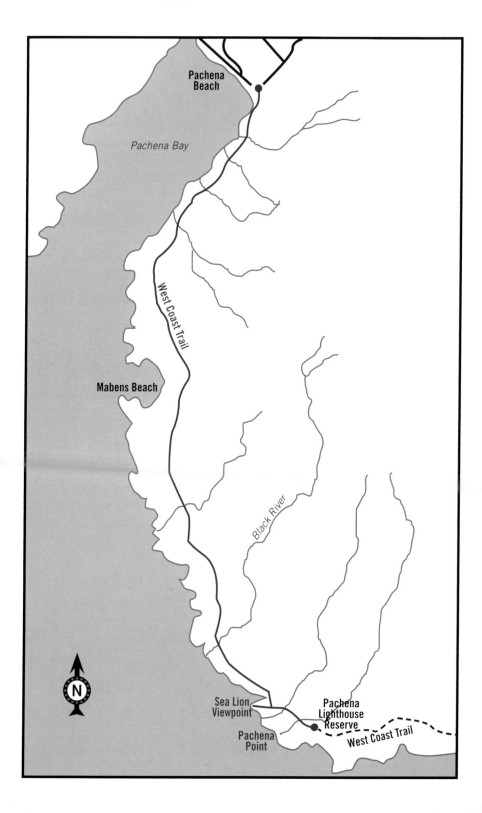

to the water's edge along this section to explore some of the shore life.

4. After crossing a small stream, the trail gradually rises and angles slightly away from the shore. A little beyond 4 km the route passes parallel with, but not close to, a sandy bay. Exploring this bay requires a considerable descent down a rough track through thick bush, since the trail is about 100 m above the shore.

5. After descending slightly, the trail runs through a small First Nation reserve, though you will see little evidence of this. Along this section of the coast and the rest of the way to Pachena Point, the route passes the sites of four major ship disasters, three of which involved considerable loss of life. The trail is away from the shore, however, and, in any case, the wrecks are hidden from view. At 8 km you will cross the Black River (actually a stream) via a bridge.

6. A little past 9 km, turn right down a signposted side path for a spectacular viewing spot for Steller sea lions. Often hundreds of these animals cover the large rocks below various high viewpoints on a fairly precipitous headland. From here it is possible to scramble down a narrow path onto the slabs of the rocky foreshore. This makes a fascinating area to explore, but be wary of slippery rocks and rogue waves.

7. Return to the main trail and complete the trip to Pachena Point lighthouse. From the grounds of the lighthouse you can enjoy another high viewpoint. Particularly notice the cable down the cliff to the shore for hauling supplies up the vertiginous cliffs.

8. Return the way you came.

ABOVE *From the clifftop viewspot over the sea lions, it is possible to scramble down a steep but safe route onto the shore.* (7)

RIGHT *Pachena Point lighthouse.* (8)

3. BOTANY BAY AND BOTANICAL BEACH

Famous for its striking, basin-like tide pools full of colourful sea life. Convoluted shoreline over three adjoining beaches, rocky headlands, cliffs and fantastically twisted trees along the shoreline path. Best viewed when the tide is at least partly out and the pools are exposed. (Tide tables are available online and posted at the trailhead.)

2.5 km (plus shorewalking and several possible kilometres along Juan de Fuca Trail)	Easy
Starting elevation: 25 m, dropping to sea level	All seasons (a few muddy spots in wet weather)

Start: Turning in to Port Renfrew from Highway 14, stay on the main route (Cerantes Road) through town and follow it to the very end. Before Cerantes Road ends you will pass a trail to Mill Bay, an interesting short route you may wish to explore before or after visiting Botanical Beach.

Difficulty: Mostly well-groomed, carefully engineered trails with a few sturdy bridges and sets of stairs. Exploring the famous tide pools requires being somewhat sure-footed if the shore is slippery (especially in winter and spring).

1. The triangle trail can be done in either direction, but this description is written for a counter-clockwise loop. Start at the signposted trailhead at the right side of the parking area. The gradual descent to the shore, mostly along an old roadbed lined with second-growth mixed trees, is not very interesting but passes quickly. Expect a few muddy patches during winter and spring.

2. Pass through a clearing with various signs, and take a long

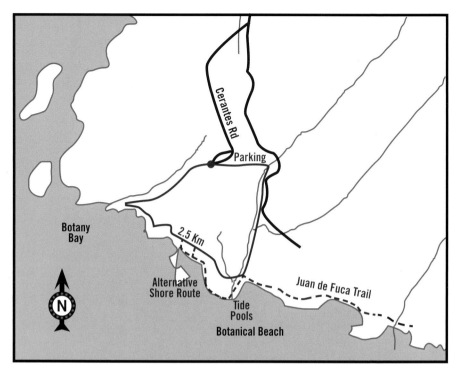

flight of sturdy wooden stairs down to a small cove. This is called "Botany Bay," largely as a sly reference to the famous bay in Australia and as echo of the much more famous "Botanical Beach" farther along the shore. Though less distinctive than Botanical Beach, this spot is well worth visiting and exploring. The views of a miniature treed islet and the heavily indented rocky shoreline are beautiful.

3. Climb back up the stairs and turn right along the shoreline trail. This path, with its fantastically twisted trees, is largely wide and level, set back among the trees.

4. After a few minutes the route comes close to the upper shore of a second bay. You can take either of the short dirt tracks onto the shore to enjoy the views. The upper shore here is sandy, while the lower is fairly rugged, rocky outcropping with some interesting tide pools. If the tide is out far enough, you can start your shorewalk to the Botanical Bay tide pools around the headland from here, but in

doing so you would miss part of the beautiful trail. Note that the posted sign indicating this to be an "escape trail" to Botanical Beach is intended to warn against trying to round the headland along the shore if the tide is high.

5. From this point the trail runs parallel to a streambed and crosses over two bridges to end at the main entrance to Botanical Beach. The striking, basin-like pools pock the flat sedimentary rock beyond the cliffy headland directly out from this spot. If you are going to explore the tide pools, you may wish to walk onto the shore after the first bridge. From this point you need to ford only one stream flowing across the shore in order to reach the best pools. If the stream is full, it is easiest to cross at the uppermost part of the beach, since the boulders lower down are generally slippery.

6. If you make your way out to the pools, you will soon see why this beach is considered "botanical." The deeply scooped-out pools are like miniature aquariums, rich with brightly coloured life. Even the upper pools have pink coralline algae, emerald surf grass and deep-blue mussels. In many of the lower ones you will also see, among other creatures, nearly fluorescent lime-green anemones and large red sea urchins.

7. Climbing up the sloping trail from the main entrance to the beach you will come to an open area and signs marking this as the beginning of the Juan de Fuca Marine Trail. Running for 47 km, this backpacking route is rugged for much of its length.

8. The first half of the last leg of the triangular trail is a straightforward trek up a fairly undistinguished road. When you reach a service area, the track narrows considerably and swings sharply left. From here to the parking lot, it winds attractively through interesting vegetation.

OPTIONS

Add several kilometres of easy trail walking by turning onto the Juan de Fuca Marine Trail shortly after you leave Botanical Beach. The trailhead is well signposted. This first part of the way is generally well graded and level, with few significant changes in elevation. Be warned, though, that if you plan a major out-and-back along this trail, it does become muddy and strenuous farther south.

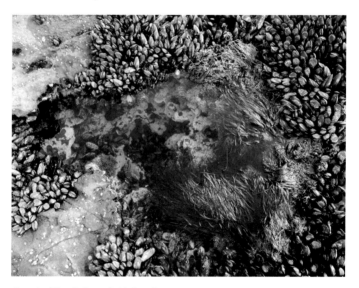

A typical bowl-shaped tidal pool.

4. PARKINSON CREEK

A taste of the famous 47-km wilderness trail at its most iso-
lated and rugged, combining rough sections of roots and steep
descents with shorewalking along solid rock outcroppings.

2 km return (plus several more possible)	Moderate
Starting elevation: 40 m, dropping to sea level	All seasons

Start: At 6 km southeast of Port Renfrew along Highway 14, you will see large signs indicating the Parkinson Creek trail-head. A narrow gravel road leads about 3 km to a parking area and a clearly signposted set of trailheads. At this point the Marine Trail swings away from the coast and cuts across this old logging road.

Difficulty: Easy at first, after angling toward the coast, the trail gradually descends a high bank, becoming increasingly difficult toward the bottom and requiring climbing over some fallen logs and skirting some mudholes. Access to the shore is possible at several points but requires a little scrambling.

There are two trailheads here, since the Marine Trail crosses the parking area. The option to the right (north-west), described here, allows you to get onto the shore most easily and quickly.

1. The trail begins as an abandoned logging road through small alders and passes over a sturdy logging-truck bridge with good views of the pretty rapids and falls of Parkinson Creek.

2. Turn down the signposted fork to the left and, a little far-ther along at another signposted fork (though the wrong trail is largely overgrown), turn right. The trail narrows considerably here and passes under a dark section of

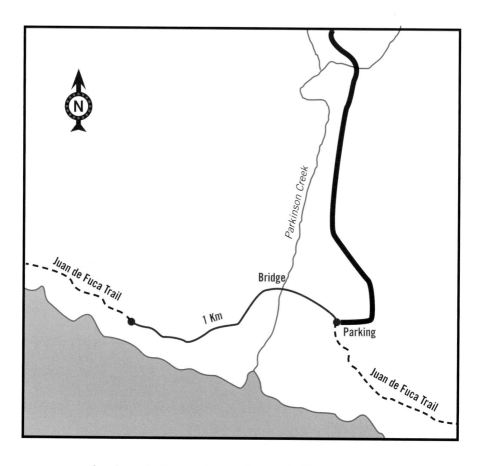

closely packed second-growth trees before emerging into the brighter, more open forest near the top of the bank.

3. The route runs along the high bank through a chest-high hedge of salal (typical of much of the Juan de Fuca Trail) before angling down toward the shore. This is the roughest section, requiring some nimble climbing over and around roots and (except after a long dry spell) mudholes. There are some great views through the weathered trees along this desolate stretch of rugged shore exposed to Pacific storms.

4. When you come close to the shore and see a cluster of beachcombed fishing floats dangling from a tree, you

One of many logs and stumps along the trail that make walking a minor adventure. (3)

can elect to leave the trail, though you will have to scramble a little.

From here, you can go farther along the shoreline, but make sure you leave plenty of time to return if the tide is rising. The shore is made up of gradually sloping, layered rock with some rifts and tide pools, so it makes for good walking.

5. Return the way you came.

OPTION

If you wish to sample more of the Marine Trail, it is best to rejoin it about 30 m along, after a particularly wet section, where the route starts to angle up and away from the shore again. For the next kilometre or so the route stays more or less close to the shore before turning a little inland and dropping to the Payzant Creek campsite (and outhouses) about 1.5 km away.

The view from partway down the trail towards the shore. When the tide is at least partly out, the exposed shelving rocks and tidal pools make for interesting walking. (3)

5. MYSTIC BEACH

The southeastern end of the famous Juan de Fuca Marine Trail, with a broad, well-used path, a dramatic suspension bridge over a deep gorge, and an isolated beach with a spectacular waterfall.

3.8 km return (plus beachwalking)	Easy to moderate
Starting elevation: 90 m (many rises and falls en route to shore)	All seasons

Start: Some 32 km west of Sooke on Highway 14, turn off at the signposted entry to the parking lot for China Beach and Juan de Fuca Marine Trail.

Difficulty: Listed as "moderately difficult" by the local tourist agency, the trail is nevertheless quite easy. Most of the route along open forest floor has been heavily tramped and spread well beyond the official track, often detouring around muddy patches. A few sections of boardwalk and small bridges help with the wettest parts. Some find the dizzying heights of the slightly swaying suspension bridge a challenge.

1. From the parking lot signposted for the Juan de Fuca Marine Trail, the trail to Mystic Beach cuts a broad swath under a forest canopy with virtually no undergrowth. After losing altitude it climbs again almost as much and continues with some undulations.

2. About halfway to the shore you will come to the spectacular suspension bridge high above Pete Wolf Creek. Since the surface of the bridge is an open grid, the experience of crossing the deep ravine can be dizzying. Not just children but even dogs occasionally have to be carried!

3. After the bridge the trail continues its downward trend

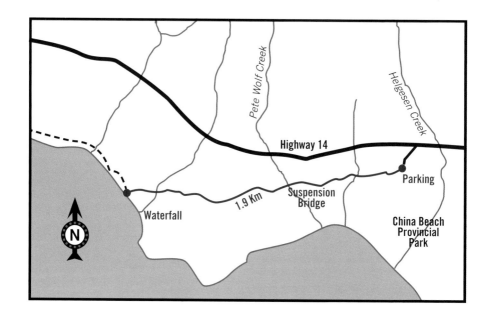

over undulations and one complex sequence of board-walks and bridges. The final descent down the high bank to the shore gives some great views along the west end of Mystic Beach and the rugged coast scenery. Notice that many of the stairs leading down the bank are actually cut into two huge spruce logs.

4. Once on the beach, you will want to visit the waterfall clearly visible a short way along the shore to the left. Although the falls can be little more than a dribble at the end of a long, dry summer, for most of the year they erupt over the cliff edge with impressive force. If the tide is out, you can explore the sandy shore of the 500-m long beach.

5. Return the way you came.

OPTION

It is possible to join the Marine Trail toward the west end of the beach and explore it for a full day's experience. At 47 rugged kilometres long, the whole trail is normally walked

The falls at the southeast end of the beach are at their most scenic in the spring or early summer. (4)

by backpackers, though ultra-marathoners occasionally attempt it in a single day. While the first section of the trail mostly runs close to the shore, occasionally dipping inland, it is 7 km until you come to an obvious day destination, namely Bear Beach. Though this section of the trail is rated "moderate" by BC Parks, it does occasionally have stretches that require a little nimbleness and balance. In fact, it seems much more than 7 km, so be prepared.

6. WHIFFIN SPIT

A geographical phenomenon: a long, winding spit extending nearly across the mouth of Sooke Basin. Views into the basin and across the Strait of Juan de Fuca as well as of the waters that swirl through the narrow gap with the rising and falling tide.

2.5 km return	Easy
Elevation throughout: sea level	All seasons

Start: From central Sooke, take Highway 14 toward Port Renfrew. On the outskirts of Sooke, 1.7 km from the central traffic lights, turn left onto Whiffin Spit Road. Park in the signposted parking area at the end of this road.

Difficulty: A broad, even path of crushed gravel runs the entire length of the spit, passable even with (sturdy) baby strollers. An optional, user-made loop trail around the perimeter of the comparatively broad, tree-covered formation at the far end of the spit is a little more difficult, requiring some careful footing among loose rocks and climbing over a few logs.

1. The trail could hardly be easier to find or more difficult to stray from. The first section, some of it reinforced with rough boulders creating the appearance of a causeway or breakwater, is barely wider than the track itself. Time your visit to coincide with high water if you want to experience the sensation of being on a mere sliver of land reaching far out into the basin. At low tide, in contrast, you have the option of exploring some of the gravelly beaches that slope gradually away from both sides of the spit.

2. As you near the end of the spit, you will find that it gradually broadens and that the entire end of it has groves of windswept firs and some small, user-made cross-trails (as well as an outhouse). Rather than simply returning the

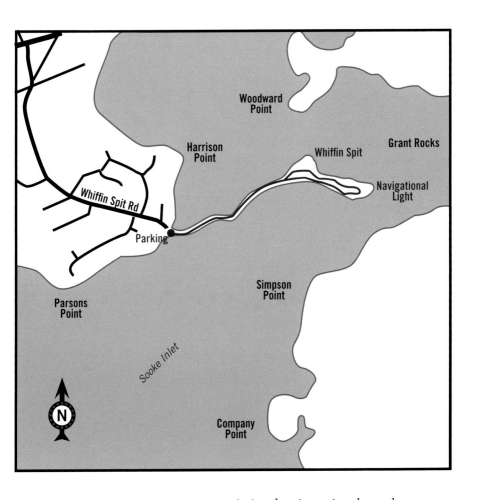

way you came, you can maximize the viewpoints by making a circuit of this final section of the spit. Walk almost to the large navigational light and cut across the island to find a narrow, winding but generally clear path. The track is mostly close to the uppermost section of shore, though occasionally it wanders behind the logs that line the shore and at other points leads down to a band of egg-like rocks covering the upper beach. The trail peters out as the land narrows, so you will have to rejoin the wide trail you used on the way in. Alternatively, as you will no doubt see, some visitors walk primarily on the shore, though the going is considerably slower that way.

ABOVE *The broad path runs along the top of the reinforced gravel spit towards East Sooke. (1)*

RIGHT *The view east across part of Sooke Basin towards the Sooke Hills. (1)*

7. IRON MINE BAY

Easy, forested trail under some large firs and coastal spruce to a pebbly pocket beach and rugged headlands. Great views of the Olympic Mountains. Options for longer walks along cliffs and bluffs of East Sooke Park Coast Trail.

4.5-km loop (with longer and shorter options)	Easy (with moderate and strenuous options)
Starting elevation: 45 m, dropping to sea level	All seasons

Start: From Highway 1 at 8 km north of Victoria, take exit 10 toward Colwood. Drive 3.5 km south along the Old Island Highway noting that it changes name to Sooke Road at the traffic lights. After 16 km turn left onto Gillespie Road for 5.6 km. Turn right onto East Sooke Road for 8 km and left onto Pike Road until the sign for Iron Mine Bay.

Difficulty: The main route to Iron Mine Bay could hardly be easier. Generally even and wide, the crushed gravel path slopes gradually and evenly toward the shore, with only a slightly steeper dirt section immediately above the beach. The side trail to the Pike Point viewpoint is more rugged and requires passing over some bare rock. Ventures south along the Coast Trail involve light scrambling over rocky bluffs and careful footing along cliff edges.

1. The first part of the route is down a gradually sloping, wide track running parallel to a small stream on one side and some interesting fern-hung bluffs on the other. Notice a few huge old stumps with notches dating from the earliest logging days. When you see a sign indicating "Viewpoint," turn right.

2. The trail at first is easy, then it narrows considerably as it leads toward the shore through ferns. As you approach

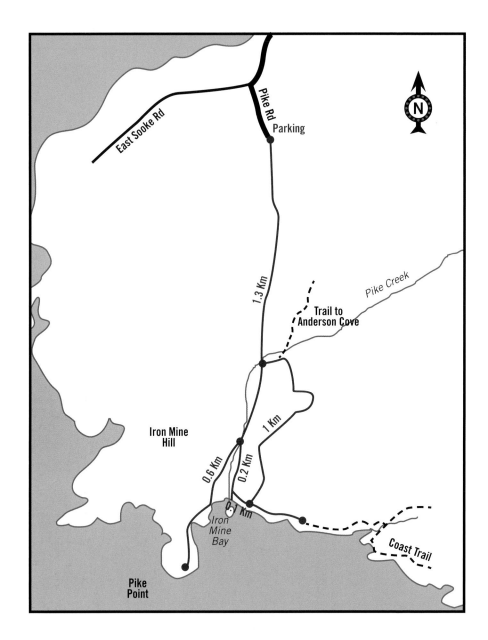

the water, with glimpses of Iron Mine Bay, you will see another sign for the viewpoint and a warning about "steep cliffs" and the need to supervise children. Turn right onto this trail. From this point on, the path will require a little care and nimbleness as you climb up onto a headland of mossy bluffs. The views are lovely, especially of the Olympic Mountains and Secretary Island just offshore, but they are largely framed by trees.

3. Return to the junction with the main Iron Mine trail and follow this smooth, easy route to the shore. An interesting interpretive sign provides some history of the spot. Once you reach the exquisite little pocket beach, with its polished pebbles, you can rest and soak in the view framed by the jagged headlands and windblown trees or you can clamber along the user-made trails over the islet to the left.

4. From this little beach you have the option of walking some distance down the East Sooke Coast Trail. The whole route requires several hours, however, and is best done by arranging to have a shuttle vehicle at the other end. For a fairly short sample of this spectacularly beautiful trail, follow the track over several high, rocky bluffs and along some cliff-edge sections for about 500 m until you see a user-made trail leading away from the main trail down to a grassy, level area and an excellent viewpoint of a jagged little islet. Since hikers regularly get lost on the Coast Trail, the secret to keeping on track is always to keep an eye out for small orange rectangles. If you go more than, say, 50 m without seeing one, retrace your steps until you see one and take a more well-beaten route.

5. After your exploration down the Coast Trail, return almost to Iron Mine Bay until you see a sign for Mt. Maguire. Although you can go past this sign and simply retrace the easy trail from the bay to your car, for the loop route turn right onto this Mt. Maguire trail. The track begins by climbing over mossy knolls and through sprinkled trees before levelling a little and entering

deeper forests (where, in April, you may spot some lady's slippers). The trail winds first up a trough between ridges, then climbs onto the west ridge before running along its crest and dropping down to a bit of table land. The descent to a T-junction is comparatively steep.

6. Counterintuitively, turn left at this junction (signposted to the right for Mt. Maguire and Anderson Cove). This branch leads back a short way to the main Iron Mine Bay / Pike Road trail. Turn right to return to your vehicle.

OPTIONS

Because East Sooke Park is interlaced with trails (many of them actually old roadbeds), you can hike through dozens of combinations of routes. Most of the junctions are well signposted but can be confusing if you don't have a map of the whole park. A good loop from the opposite end of the park, Aylard Farm, is described separately in the next chapter. A good hiking loop largely away from the water is described in the companion volume, *Popular Day Hikes 4: Vancouver Island*.

OPPOSITE *Iron Mine beach seen from the perspective of the islet on the southeast end of the beach. (3)*

LEFT *The Coast Trail beyond Iron Mine Bay has several sections requiring light scrambling. (4)*

BELOW *The signpost and trail junction leading to Pike Point viewpoint. (2)*

8. AYLARD FARM TO BEECHEY HEAD

East Sooke Park

An historic farm field, a small but lovely sandy beach and low, rocky outcrops along garden-like scatterings of twisted pine and arbutus beside the sea. An ancient petroglyph and high sea bluffs, concluding with a shaded roadbed with large firs and swordferns.

5.8-km loop (longer and shorter options)	Easy first and last part; moderately difficult central part
Starting elevation: 10 m High point: 90 m, with many small ups and downs	All seasons (Aylard meadow is wet in winter and spring)

Start: Turn off Highway 1 onto Millstream Road and follow it for 3.2 km as it turns into Veterans Memorial Parkway / Highway 14. Turn right onto Sooke Road (Highway 14) for 13.2 km, then left onto Gillespie Road. After 5.6 km, turn left onto East Sooke Road for 2 km. The first right turn, Becher Bay Road, ends just less than 1 km later at East Sooke Park Aylard Farm parking lot.

Difficulty: Much of the route is easy, along broad, level paths with little change in elevation. One option allows a short loop along equally easy trails. The route described here does involve about 2 km of moderately difficult climbing up and down rocky bluffs. Though the trail is much used, it is possible to wander off on side routes and even become lost. It is important to follow the orange rectangles, usually attached to the rocks. If you go more than 50 m without seeing one of these, retrace your route until you do see one and take a more promising path. There are many branching trails, but the significant ones are well signposted.

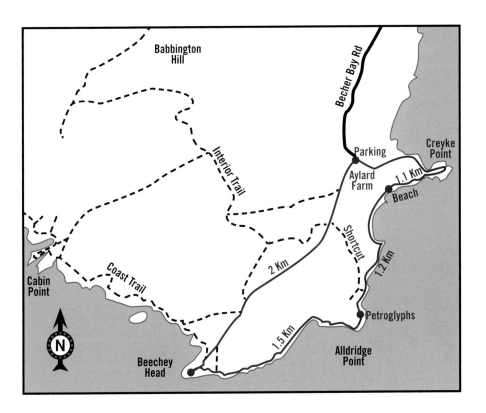

1. First walk straight toward the water until you see a sign pointing to Creyke Point at the end of the meadow. Turn left to follow the path toward Becher Bay. This trail follows the shore of the bay before leading along a narrow isthmus to Creyke Point itself. Take the path left onto the rocky knolls (you may see rock climbers on the sea cliffs), before following the path along the outer coast toward the beach below a meadow. You may wish to visit this 100-m long beach, since it is the only sandy one in the park.

2. Leave the beach and follow the trail through the forest as it curves around the bay toward the first headland. A parallel track runs along the edge of the meadow immediately above and joins the forest trail. From this point on, the path starts to rise and fall a little over largely

smooth bluffs until you reach the Alldridge Point petroglyphs (only one of which is easy to see). Note the sign
on your right just before the petroglyph pointing out
the optional shortcut loop back to Aylard Farm. To view
the petroglyph, climb down onto the boulders of the
upper shore and look back at the smooth rock face. An
interpretive sign on the path provides interesting information about this and other petroglyphs.

3. Immediately after the petroglyph, the route becomes
   more difficult. In fact, a sign posted here warns you
   of steep cliffs ahead. There is no real danger, but you
   should be prepared for a little huffing and puffing as you
   climb up and over various bluffs. The trail from here to
   Beechey Head passes some amazingly contorted trees
   and occasionally dips inland before emerging to striking
   viewpoints on the increasingly cliffy coastline.

4. As you near Beechey Head, the highest point on this
   trail, you will see a sign to Aylard Farm. (You could turn
   right here to begin your homeward trip.) Go a little farther on the Coast Trail to reach the crest of the trail and
   the short side route to the Beechey Head viewpoint. Be
   aware that this whole promontory is criss-crossed with
   user-made trails.

5. After absorbing the striking views, return to the Coast
   Trail and find the first signposted trail for Aylard Farm.
   Three Aylard Farm trails converge a short distance inland.
   The inland route begins with a significant climb through
   open fir forest over mossy rocks. Within a few minutes
   you will come to additional converging trails, with several signs pointing to Cabin Point and other destinations. Again turn right, to follow the Aylard Farm Path.

6. All the way to the parking lot, you will be following old
   roadbeds. Pass three intersections with signs pointing to

ABOVE *Typical of the many wildly twisted arbutus between the petroglyph and Beechey Head.* (3)

BELOW *The petroglyph, usually interpreted as a sea monster.* (2)

the left and to the Inland Trail. The second will also point rightward toward the petroglyphs. As you approach the trailhead you may be tempted to shortcut across the meadows rather than carry on straight ahead through the trees on the roadbed. While both routes will clearly take you back to the parking lot, be aware that the meadows can be squelchy well into May.

OPTIONS

There are dozens of different routes possible, since all of East Sooke Park is a maze of trails. The following two are the most highly recommended.

1. Carry on past Beechey Head to Cabin Point. This part of the trail drops and rises several times, at one point going past a striking little islet. At Cabin Point itself there are interesting interpretive posters about the historic fisherman's cabin the point is named for. Two trails lead inland and uphill from here to the Interior Trail. In both cases, turn right at the T-junction onto this trail, which leads over a crest and then drops to join the first of three roughly parallel tracks, all leading left to Aylard Farm.

2. If you can arrange a shuttle vehicle, consider doing the whole Coast Trail, a significant day's adventure but well worth the logistical issues. Technically only 10 km long, it feels much longer. In addition, check out the loop trail from the other end, described separately as Walk 7, Iron Mine Bay.

9. WITTY'S LAGOON

Many diverse elements to enjoy here: an enclosed lagoon sur-
rounded by some huge Douglas firs and arbutus, an elegant
waterfall, and a long, pristine sandy beach backed by a dune-
like spit. Striking views of the Olympic Mountains and Race
Rocks lighthouse.

4.5 km return (plus beachwalking)	Easy
Starting elevation: 20 m, many gentle undulations to sea level	All seasons (muddy patches winter and spring)

Start: From Highway 1, turn onto Millstream Road south and continue straight ahead onto Veterans Memorial Parkway (Highway 14) for 5.8 km. Turn left onto Latoria Road for 1.7 km, then right onto Metchosin Road for 2.3 km. You next want Duke Road, but be sure to take the second turn onto this loop road. After 650 m on Duke Road, turn right, onto Olympic View Drive, for 200 m. If you have difficulty parking along the shoulder (though it is broad), there is a parking lot for a nearby park 200 m back, near the junction with Olympic View Drive. Although the main entrance to the park is farther along Metchosin Road, this small, relatively obscure entrance is better for starting a long, satisfying walk. It is also possible to drive close to the main beach from Witty's Lagoon Road off Metchosin Road.

Difficulty: The trail has been upgraded with bridges, guard-rails and reinforced paths so that, apart from a few muddy sections in winter and spring, it is suitable for nearly all levels of ability.

1. Ignore the small directional sign pointing to "Witty's Lagoon" 50 m before the end of the road. This is merely a route to a public access. Walk to the end of the road, where you will see two equally broad trails. The one on

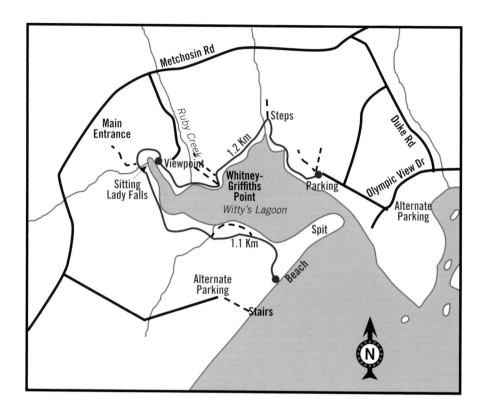

the right is marked as a horse trail. Take the trail on the left and begin your gradual descent through a fir forest toward the northeast shore of the lagoon. Ignore a trail to the right signposted for Duke Road. Near the shore you will pass many wildly contorted arbutus. Time your visit for mid to high tide to see the lagoon at its most attractive and richest with bird life. Low tide exposes mostly mud flats. Along the north shore of the lagoon you will pass a park bench and see some wonderful views across the still waters to Witty's Spit and the Olympic Mountains.

2. As you cross a small bridge over a pretty little cascading brook, you will see a set of wood and gravel steps leading up to the right. Note that you may wish to turn up here on your return trip. From this bridge the trail follows

the northwest shore. Ignore all paths to the right, sticking always to the lagoon. Make sure you don't miss the trail down to Whitney-Griffiths Point, where you can find a picnic table and washrooms as well as an especially lovely, though very enclosed, view. Cross another pretty bridge, over Ruby Creek.

3. The lagoon-side trail rises as you approach Sitting Lady Falls. A sign warns of "Steep Cliffs." After theorizing on the source of the name of these split falls (most dramatic from late autumn to spring), you will find the trail cutting inland to the base of a service road, where you will find more washrooms and a "teaching shelter." The trail goes even farther inland, passing through signposted private property (belonging to an adjacent school). Ignore the trail and sign on your right, to "Nature Centre Parking," and come out again to the falls and the bridge directly over them.

4. The trail drops to run next to the water along the south shore of the lagoon. When you cross over a marshy little stream the route splits for a short distance. The trail to the left is more attractive but does have a very muddy section in the wet season. The final section to Witty's Beach is level and low. You will emerge on a splendid expanse of silver sand, stretching out well over 100 m at low tide. There are more washrooms here and a picnic table.

5. After wandering out over the sand flats and/or walking to the end of the spit, return the way you came.

OPTIONS

1. On your return trip you can cut across the trail above Whitney-Griffiths Point and again above the first bridge. Neither of these routes is as attractive as the lagoon-side trail, however.

2. Once back to your vehicle, you may wish to visit the adjacent Tower Point Park, at the junction of Olympic Park Drive and Duke Road. You can make a 1-km loop through this park, which has beautiful views from the rocky bluffs over several tiny islets.

RIGHT *One of many magnificent arbutus along the trail.*

BELOW *The view southeast along the spit. Picnic facilities and informational signs are located in this prime beach spot. (4)*

10. MACAULAY POINT

An exposed, picturesquely bleak promontory, small beach, marina and breakwater. Historic bunkers and great views of the Olympic Mountains.

2 km	Easy
Starting elevation: near sea level	All seasons

Start: From Highway 1 at a set of traffic lights 2 km north of central Victoria, turn onto Tillicum Road for 1.6 km. Take a slight jog left onto Craigflower Road for 100 m and then the first right onto Lampson Street for 2.3 km. Turn right onto Munro Street and almost immediately left where you see two signs, one for Buxton Green, Macaulay Point, the other for Fleming Beach boat ramp.

Difficulty: The paths are smooth and easy. If you leave the trail to go down to the small cove with rocky beach, walk along the breakwater or otherwise explore the shore off the trail, you will have to be a little careful with your footing. Be particularly cautious in winter, when the rocks can be slippery.

1. From the parking lot by the marina, head left along the raised concrete walkway, which curves behind a small beach. If you want to include a visit to the beach on your trip here, plan to arrive when the tide is mostly in so that only the sugary dry sand of the upper beach is exposed. The low-tide rocks are largely jagged and slimy.

2. Carry on along the edge of the grassy picnic area immediately beyond the beach. Oddly, the concrete pathway narrows to about 50 cm (20 in.) along the outer perimeter of this picnic area. If you are feeling sure-footed you can scramble up a bit of rock to rejoin the main trail. Otherwise, complete the circuit of the picnic area to link to the main trail.

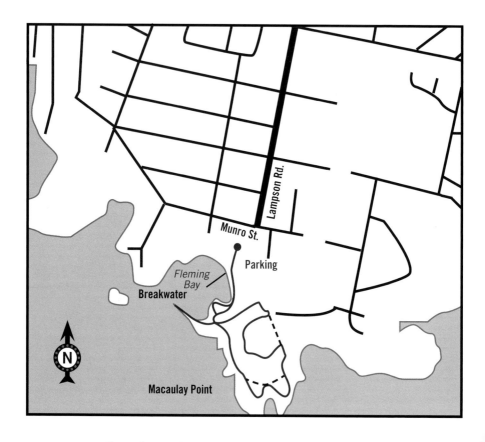

3. Follow the trail to the breakwater. Walk the length of the breakwater for interesting views and return to the shorefront trail.

4. Branch right just beyond the orientation sign and map. Ignore each of the next four trails leading left in order to keep close to the shore. (These branches are only short-cuts along the base of two promontories.) After the first promontory and immediately behind an islet, you can scramble onto the shore, where there is a small beach with wave-rounded rocks. Along this section you will find your view changes significantly from looking across Esquimalt Harbour to the entrance to Victoria Harbour.

5. The trail leads behind a small thicket of bushes to climb

gently inland. When you come to a road-width concrete track, turn left and immediately left again to pass the first of two long-abandoned military bunkers. This is a reminder that in fact this whole area, militarized in the late 19th century, is leased from the Department of National Defence.

6. Continue beneath high hedges to circle clockwise to the high point of the park and the second bunker. Turn left at the next two junctions.

7. The last section of trail descends gently toward the shore and the starting point of the circuit walk. Return past the small harbour to the parking lot.

The central part of the main loop passes above two small coves that are attractive to explore, especially at low tide.

11. ISLAND VIEW REGIONAL PARK

A loop trail starting through a low, bushy area amongst dunes at the back of a narrow beachfront park and returning along the upper edge of a sandy, log-strewn shoreline. Lovely views of James Island and Sidney Island sand cliffs, D'Arcy Island and several American Gulf Islands.

2.7 km, plus beachwalking option to Cordova Spit Park	Easy
Elevation throughout: sea level	All seasons

Start: Driving toward Sidney from Victoria on Highway 14, turn right onto Island View Road (at a traffic light) and simply follow the road to its end as it snakes down a bluff toward sea level. Park, if possible, in the first lot you come to, directly ahead at the end of the road, since this is the best place to begin your walk. Either this parking lot or a second one, down Homathko Road to your left, will do.

Difficulty: For the most part this is a broad and well-maintained path of crushed gravel with almost no change in altitude. If you choose to walk at least part of the loop along the beach itself, be aware that the logs that line the beach can become slippery in wet weather and can sometimes roll out from under you.

1. From the first lot, the route leads from a trailhead near the shore and runs parallel to the shoreline along the edge of the most used part of the park. Here you will see a covered picnic shelter, outhouses and picnic tables.

2. The trail next passes a peculiar camping area, open only during the summer. A large, open, grassy area, it is subdivided by serpentine split-cedar fencing. Shortly past

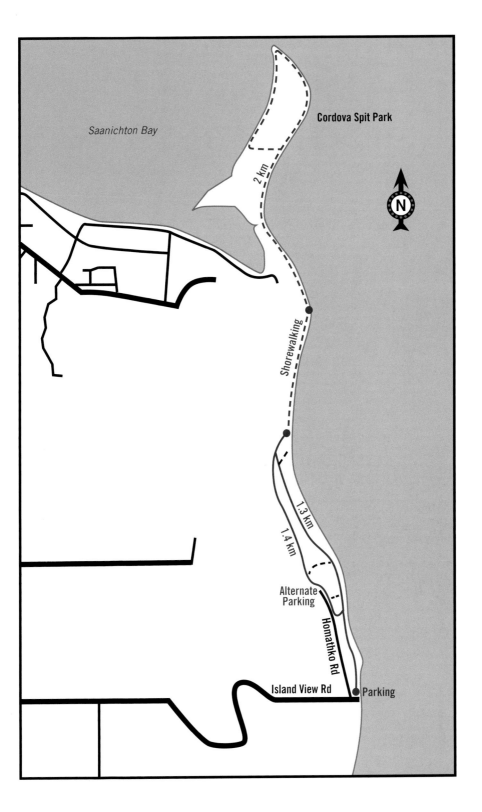

Saanichton Bay

Cordova Spit Park

2 km

Shorewalking

1.3 km

1.4 km

Alternate
Parking

Homathko Rd

Island View Rd   Parking

N

this section, take the first trail away from the shore (though there is more than one, all serving the same purpose). Turn right, onto Homathko Road. When you come to the end of this road, carry on straight ahead down a broad, level track through thickets of low bush. Ignore the broad trail to the right leading back to the shore and a smaller trail on the left leading inland through fields.

3. The trail winds past an interesting marshy area before curving toward the shore along the edge of another split-cedar fence. A sign indicates that the area behind the fence has been closed to allow vegetation to recover. The surroundings appear increasingly dune-like as the trail becomes sandier and a little unstable under-foot. You will see a sign indicating that you have come to end of the park and the boundary of the Tsawout First Nation. Although various activities are forbidden beyond this point – including dogs – walking is not, as long as you exercise caution.

4. Retrace your route a few metres along the sandy trail parallel to the fence until you see a broad trail to your left running parallel to the shore and about 20 m back from it.

5. After the first section, the trail climbs to the top of a dune-like ridge immediately behind the beach and stays there. Partway back you will rejoin the section of trail that began your circuit and follow it back to the beginning.

OPTIONS

1. Although various options are open to you here, the rec-ommended route takes you down to the shore itself and along the upper beach past the Tsawout Reserve, at least

ABOVE *A suggested turnaround point along the shore northwest of the main park. One of the only rocky outcroppings on a beach of pebbles and sand. Salt Spring Island is visible beyond the tip of Saanich Peninsula. (O)*

LEFT *The weathered split-cedar fence near the north end of the inland trail toward the shore. (3)*

as far as the end of the curve of shoreline that ends in a small area of rocky outcropping.

2. Rather than walk both directions on trails, you can of course go along the beach instead. At low tide you can kick off your shoes, though you may do better with sandals for some gravelly sections.

3. Carry on past the recommended turnaround rocky outcropping and follow the curve of the next bay to reach Cordova Spit Municipal Park. In fact, for anyone wishing to visit this park and experience the bird-spotting opportunities that are its chief feature, this is the best route. The reserve land adjoining it has no public roads through it. Distance from Island View Park along the shore: 700 m each way. Circuit of Cordova Spit Park: 2.6 km.

The route begins and ends at a large, grassy field with a picnic shelter and other facilities. (1)

12. MCKENZIE BIGHT

A descending gully of large, moss-hung trees, a rocky shoreline of sun-baked, twisted arbutus and a pretty waterfall by the ascending return route.

6.2-km loop	Moderate
Starting elevation: 140 m Low point: sea level	All seasons

Start: Turn off the Patricia Bay Highway about 8 km north of central Victoria, taking exit 11 onto Royal Oak Drive. After 500 m, turn left onto Royal Oak Drive / BC Highway 17A for 750 m, then left onto Wallace Drive for 500 m. Next, turn left onto Willis Point Road, and after 4 km and merging onto Ross Durrance Road for another 500 m, you will see several signs and a parking lot.

Difficulty: The trail is generally well maintained and even. Boardwalks and bridges help with otherwise wet crossings. The only cautionary note is for those not expecting a little moderate exercise on the return leg of the loop.

This loop can be done in either direction, though counter-clockwise is probably better.

1. From the parking lot, cross the road and begin down the broad, even track. Don't be too concerned by the sign a little later that says "Caution: Steep Terrain and Cliffs." The trail itself is easy and smooth. The roadbed descends through mossy maples and firs parallel to a stream to arrive at a gravelly shoreline. This indented part of the coast with its low-tide expanse of shore is the "bight."

2. Note the small bridge to your left for your return journey. For now, turn right and ascend to a treed promontory. At

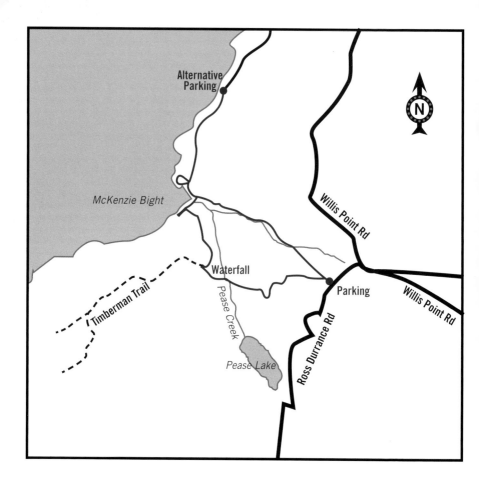

this point it is worthwhile leaving the road-width main trail to explore the small side trails over the promontory.

3. Return to the main trail, where you will find an outhouse. The track takes you away from the water's edge, rising about 35 m before descending back to the shoreline through a set of switchbacks.

4. Along this shoreline section, you may wish to leave the main track to explore two picturesque little promontories, the second with a small, pebbly beach suitable for picnicking.

5. To complete the route, go the remaining 200 m to the

ABOVE *An imposing arbutus, framing the view along Saanich Inlet at the first headland. (2)*

LEFT *The falls viewed from the side of a deep gorge, most of the way up the returning part of the loop. (6)*

end of the trail, where there is a parking lot, but since this section is well above the shoreline, you may prefer to turn back once you've reached this pretty promontory and beach.

6. When you have retraced your route to the bridge, cross it and in a short distance head uphill along the signposted "Cascade Trail." This section, following the course of a gorge, is by far the steepest. At some points, a wooden safety railing runs beside the trail. As you approach the steepest part of the track you will get a good view of the "cascade" after which the route is named. If you are lucky and the creek is high, the falls are spectacular.

7. A short distance above the falls you will come to a junction. The right fork leads to the long and moderately strenuous trail ending at the Caleb Pike Trailhead. To return to your vehicle, turn left onto Timberman Trail and follow the nearly level, road-width track back to the paved road (Durrance Lake Road).

8. Turn left along the paved road. After 100 m you will come to the parking lot.

OPTION

If you are thinking about adding some distance by exploring the trail that leads to the right just above the falls, be aware that it climbs steadily uphill and does not give you a good view until you have gone almost 2 km. Still, it is a pleasant walk through increasingly open forest.

13. MILL BAY NATURE PARK

A fairly short sequence of intersecting trails in a beautiful fir and cedar forest sloping toward the tidal flats at the head of Mill Bay.

1.1 km (with options)	Easy
Starting elevation: 18 m High point: 32 m	All seasons

Start: A little north of Mill Bay, turn east onto Kilmalu Road for 1.5 km, then right, onto Hollings Road, until you come to the well-signposted nature park on your right. The parking lot is actually a loop with a structure for a portable washroom (currently empty) at the tip of the loop.

Difficulty: Minor changes in elevation aside, this could hardly be an easier route. Bridges and viewing platforms are among the improvements to the trail that make the going easy. All ascents are gradual and all paths are wide and clear. As you will see from the posted map of the park, you can wind your way through various sequences of intersecting trails. Recommended is the circuit route described here.

1. Begin your circuit by getting your geographical bearings. Retrace the route you took into the parking lot by walking to Hollings Road and following it to the water's edge. A short flight of stairs takes you to a rough gravel shore with some rocky outcroppings. Low tide exposes a large area of tidal flats with a stream wandering through sticky sand.

2. After exploring as much of the beach as you feel inclined, retrace your steps back toward the parking lot and turn

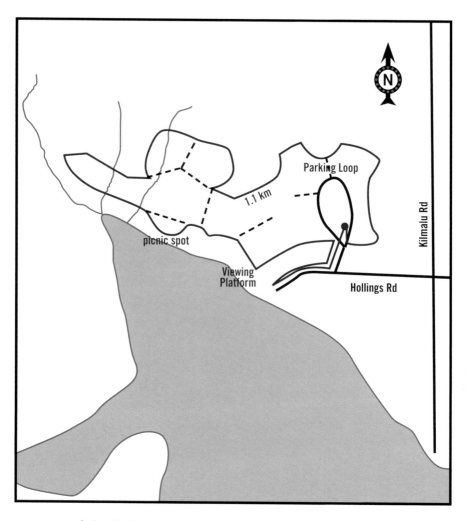

left off the trail, cutting across the entrance road to the parking loop. The broad path will take you through tall firs and cedars to a bank slightly above the shore and a solidly built wooden wildlife-viewing platform with handrails.

3. Turn back from the viewing platform and head along the trail parallel to the shore, keeping left, until you come to a side trail on your left allowing you to descend slightly to a level picnic area near the shore and, just beyond this, a bridge crossing a small creek.

The picnic area with easy access to the tidal flat and its many interesting creatures flourishing in the slightly muddy sand. (3)

4. The trail turns inland and, after a short distance, climbs the bank via a sturdy set of plank-and-earth steps.

5. At the next junction, turn left to reach the highest point of the park and the edge of the forest, with a farm field visible through the trees. From here the trail crosses another bridge and stays more or less high, traversing the bank once you turn back again onto the main circular route.

6. Continue making left turns to keep to the outer circuit. The last part of your walk will take you above the parking area, visible through the trees, and after running parallel to the end of Hollings Road, delivers you back to the entrance road to the parking area.

One of several solid little bridges in the park, this one near the high point of the trail at the northwest end of the park. (5)

14. MANLEY CREEK PARK

A loop trail starting in a park, with bridges over a cascading, fern-lined brook. High staircases to and from a gravel shore, a meadow lane and awe-inspiring views of Mt. Baker's snowy volcanic cone.

2.25 km	Easy
Starting elevation: 42 m	All seasons

Start: From Highway 1 at about 4 km north of Mill Bay, turn east onto Hutchinson Road. Then, after 2.4 km, turn left onto Ratcliffe Road. Follow it to its end, about 1.4 km along.

Difficulty: All trails are well graded. Bridges and staircases make getting over the stream and down the bank easy. Some careful footing on the gravelly shore and a little effort in ascending a long staircase are required. The shore section is almost impassable at high tides (typical of summer evenings and winter midday).

While you can choose many routes through the maze of trails and bridges in the park at the beginning of the route, the following sequence allows you maximum variation with minimum repetition.

1. Walk past the map and outhouses, bearing left at a fork in the path to pass a picnic area on your right. After the picnic area, cross the stream via the uppermost bridge.

2. After the bridge, turn right to follow the stream, then right again to cross the creek via the middle bridge.

3. Carry on to the next junction and turn left to head farther downhill; then turn left again to cross the lowest bridge.

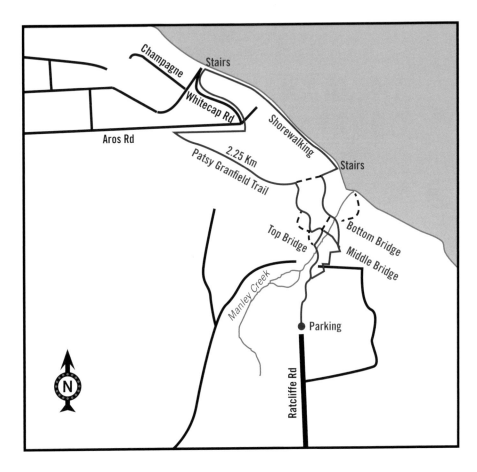

4. Turn right and head downhill until you reach a picnic area with several tables, and beyond that, a magnificent sequence of wooden staircases leading onto the gravelly shore.

5. Walk along the shore until you come to a long, wooden staircase leading up the steep, forested bank to the end of a road.

6. A short distance up this road, opposite a sign for "Champagne Drive," a well-used trail leads into a stand of small trees. About 100 m along will bring you to some yellow posts and the end of a short residential street (Whitecap Road).

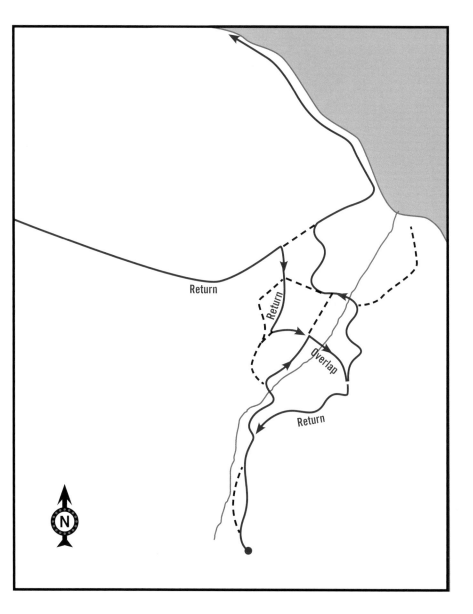

7. Turn right up Aros Road for 200 m until you see the well-signposted entrance to "Patsy Granfield Memorial Trail" on your left.

8. This lane-like trail traverses above a meadow area with magnificent views of Mt. Baker. After 400 m the trail

turns more steeply downhill and enters the edge of Manley Creek Park.

9. You can meander your way through the small-scale maze of trails and bridges to return to your vehicle. To walk primarily on trails you have not yet used, turn right, uphill, to find the middle bridge. Cross this bridge and again turn right to head largely uphill back to the park entrance.

RIGHT *This rock-solid staircase in Manley Park is one of a series providing access to the beach from the high shoreline along this stretch of coast. (5)*

BELOW *Mt. Baker, actually in the US, looks amazingly close on a clear day. Still an active volcano and permanently snow and glacier clad, the mountain holds the record for the most snowfall in the 48 contiguous states. (8)*

15. CEES AND MIEP HOF PARK

A mixed route, largely contouring down one side of a forested ravine, passing down a residential street and rejoining a natural area for the final leg to the mostly sandy beach.

1.75 km return (plus shorewalking)	Easy
Starting elevation: 62 m	All seasons

Start: On Highway 1 at 7 km south of Duncan, turn east onto Koksilah Road. After 2.5 km, go straight ahead on Cherry Point Road, turning right after 1.4 km to stay on Cherry Point Road. About 1.2 km along, on the left (north) side of the road, among trees opposite an open field, find the somewhat obscured small parking area and the interpretive park sign.

Difficulty: The trail through the ravine has been carefully built to provide an even, well-graded surface. Stairs on steep slopes reduce chances of slipping in wet weather. The return trip requires some exertion. Walking on the beach is generally easy, but water shoes or Crocs can be helpful.

1. Start along the broad, level trail of crushed gravel as it cuts along the top of one branch of the ravine then takes two large switchbacks down to a junction. To your right you will see an elaborate set of wooden stairs leading downward, and to your left a long set of wood-and-earth steps leading upward to a ridge.

2. Take the left-hand steps, pausing to look at the map posted near the base of them. Begin climbing, and once you reach the top of this ridge, contour along the trail around the end of the treed ravine. Mostly dirt, the trail is well graded, with another section of wood-and-earth steps.

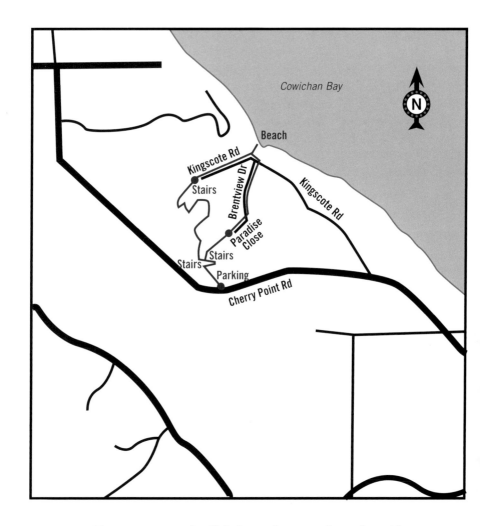

3. The route ascends slightly to the top of another ridge and an open area with a park bench. From this point to the end, the trail descends by traversing the side of the forested ravine. A final set of wood-and-earth steps brings you to Kingscote Road.

4. Walk down this road until you see the next section of the park straight ahead, with a large posted sign and map. A broad, well-maintained trail drops gradually to an attractive beach with an area of sand and logs as well as a picnic table.

5. After exploring the beach, reascend to Kingscote Road. Turn left as you walk along Kingscote Road a few steps and to the right up Brentview Drive for 400 m until the first junction. Turn right onto Paradise Close and follow it to its end 70 m along.

From the end of the cul-de-sac, climb the long flight of wooden stairs to begin the upward trail along the bottom of the ravine. The ravine ends with a climb up a winding sequence of stairs to rejoin the original trail. Turn left and walk back to your vehicle.

LEFT *The long staircase from the junction of the two trails that make up the loop. (1)*

BELOW *The view across Cowichan Bay to Salt Spring Island and Mt. Bruce. (4)*

16. MAPLE GROVE PARK AND ESTUARY

Mostly a diketop walk circling a field and bordering the Koksilah River, which flows into the broad estuary of Cowichan Bay. A bird-viewing lookout, magnificent heritage maples and good views of Mt. Tzouhalem.

3.3 km for full loop; 3 km return from viewing platform	Easy
Elevation throughout: near sea level	All seasons

Start: From Highway 1 at 3 km south of Duncan, turn left onto Cowichan Bay Road. When you come to a crossroads after 1.6 km, turn sharp right to stay on Cowichan Bay Road rather than going straight ahead onto Lochmanetz Road. Almost immediately you will see Maple Grove Park, a small parking lot and a grassy area with picnic tables.

Difficulty: This broad, even route could hardly be easier. With no variations in elevation and no slippery or rough sections, this walk can be done by virtually everyone.

1. Walk through the park under the large heritage maple trees and head left to reach a small gravel road (Lochmanetz Road).

2. After a few paces along this road, take the right fork of a raised gravel track that soon becomes a dike protecting a field on the right. A little later this dike begins to run alongside the slow-moving Koksilah River, often a good place to observe waterfowl.

3. After the dike path reaches the tidal flats of the estuary, it turns along the upper shore. At low tide the water can

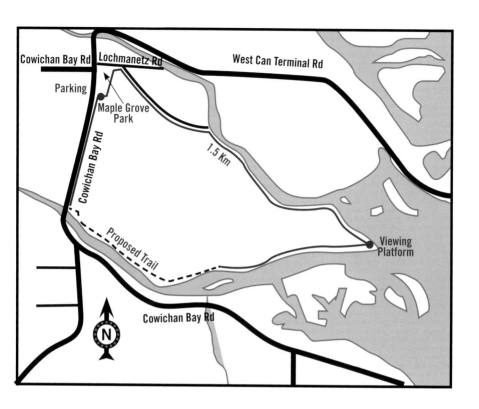

be almost a kilometre away, though at the highest tides it can come close to the dike.

4. At the end of this section of the walk, you will come to an elevated wildlife viewing platform and another stream running into the estuary. Whether or not you have brought binoculars or a camera, expect to see a wide array of shorebirds and waterfowl, including great blue herons.

5. This makes a reasonable turnaround spot, but you can continue along the dike trail away from the bay before it gradually fades out into bushy growth along the top of the dike. This part of the walk is particularly attractive because of the views across the stream to the small wooded island. Watch for red-winged blackbirds.

6. At the time of writing, the proposed trail carries along

by the edge of the field out to Cowichan Bay Road and back along the road to your starting point. Currently, a narrow beaten path runs along here. However, the trail itself is at the proposal phase of development.

RIGHT *The view back toward Cowichan Bay Road from the southern dike. Spring is a particularly beautiful time in the estuary. (5)*

BELOW *The tidal flats extending for several hundred metres across the entire head of Cowichan Bay. Across the bay, the high bluffs are part of Saltspring Island. (4)*

17. MAPLE MOUNTAIN SHORE TRAIL

Alternating areas of forest and open bluffs of moss, arbutus and oak. An isolated traversing trail with some excellent views along Sansum Narrows.

8 km return	Moderately strenuous
Starting elevation: 100 m High point: 150 m with several small ups and downs and access spots to sea level	All seasons

Start: Turn off Highway 1 onto Herd Road 3.5 km north of Duncan and follow it for 8.4 km. Turn left onto Drummond Drive for 350 m, then left onto Beaumont Avenue for 450 m. Turn right onto Arbutus Avenue and left onto Maple Mountain Road until its end. Here you will see a large oval turnaround in which to park.

Difficulty: The trail is narrow and at some points slippery in wet weather. Some sections are fairly rugged, requiring careful footing. The route is moderately strenuous, since it ascends and descends over rocky bluffs. In July and August be careful when crossing sections thick with newly fallen arbutus leaves, as they can be treacherously slippery.

1. Although there is no sign at the trailhead, a few metres along the obvious gravel track you will see a "Trail" sign and the beginning of splashes of blue on trees. For the first part of the route you will be on the "blue trail," marked with both paint and flagging tape. Later you will switch to "red" and "yellow" routes to keep close to the shore.

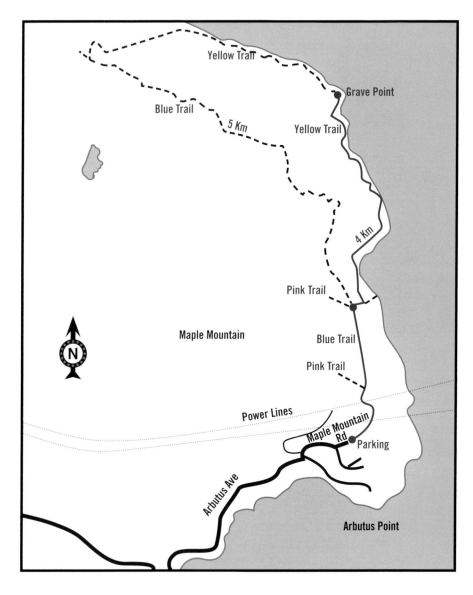

2. Cross the first of two cleared swaths carrying hydroelec-
   tric lines to Salt Spring Island, visible opposite across
   Sansum Narrows. When you reach the second set of
   power lines, the path switchbacks steeply upward to
   gain about 50 m elevation before entering the forest.

3. Once you enter the forest, be careful, as the paths here are a little confusing. To your left is one end of the "red" trail, leading to the summit of Maple Mountain. However, you can head left, then fork right onto the "blue" trail almost immediately. Alternatively, you can fork right at this first junction, heading slightly downhill, though a few dozen metres along it will merge with another version of the "blue" trail coming in from the left.

4. For the next section, this narrow trail tends downward, though with a few uphill sections. Be particularly careful where the trail traverses a narrow ledge before switch-backing down a steep slope.

5. About 1 km from the trailhead you will come to a puzzling fork where you will see a blue paint mark on a tree on the right fork, yet clearly the path is little used. In fact, this is an older route. Though passable, this right-hand route is not as good as the one that forks left. The two trails eventually converge anyway where they cross the "pink" trail a few minutes ahead.

6. Turn right and downhill to follow the "red" trail toward the shore for a short distance. After dropping 20 vertical metres, pick up the "yellow" trail contouring north along the fairly steep shoreline.

7. The trail here is mostly straightforward, but be careful when you cross clearings, since the track can be hard to spot in areas of solid rock. Always pick up a yellow splash of paint or ribbon (sometimes actually greenish yellow) before entering the trees.

8. You can gain access to the shore and small, rough beaches just under 1 km from the beginning of the "yellow" trail, but also at 1.2 km and 1.35 km. There is a particularly attractive level bluff area, Grave Point, at about

1.75 km. Any of these would make a good turnaround spot, although the large bluff is recommended, as it is a kind of visual and geographical climax to the trail.

9. Return the way you came.

OPTIONS

After this obvious bluff, the trail stays more or less close to the shoreline before gradually swinging inland. If you are feeling ambitious, you can follow this "yellow" trail until it joins the "blue" one about 2.25 km from Grave Point. Turn left onto the blue-marked mid-mountain trail and continue on it all the way to your starting point. Details of this part of the "blue" trail are in the companion volume *Popular Day Hikes 4: Vancouver Island*. This loop will add a little more than 3 km to your return trip.

In October 2013 the Cowichan Trail Stewardship Society opened a new trail up the mountain. See the web for more information.

RIGHT *A campfire spot and seats have been improvised around a tenting site at the turnaround spot.* (8)

LEFT *Though narrow, the trail is generally clear as it rises and drops over rocky knolls. (3)*

BELOW *From the second clearing that the trail crosses, the view across Sansum Narrows to Salt Spring Island. The orange and white balls are suspended from high-tension electrical wires running out to the island. (2)*

18. OSBORNE BAY PARK

A roughly circular route through a meadow, down a high bank to an arbutus-lined gravel beach and back via a heavily wooded trail with large firs and cedars.

1.75 km return plus beachwalking	Easy
Starting elevation: 38 m Low point: sea level	All seasons

Start: Follow signs from Highway 1 to Crofton, between Chemainus and Duncan. From York Avenue exiting south of Crofton (becoming Osborne Bay Road), turn left onto Adelaide Street and, just under 1 km later, go right, onto Smith Road. About 500 m along pull into the first of two gravel parking lots on your left with clearly posted signs.

Difficulty: The trails are broad and level, though the return route through the trees can be muddy and requires a little care in rooty sections.

1. Head straight across the meadow toward the ocean. The trail is sometimes a little faint in the lush – but usually mown – grass. Head over a slight rise and you will see the clear, broad continuation of the trail immediately to the right of a stand of arbutus and fir.

2. The wide, evenly graded gravel trail passes through a pleasant but unremarkable fir forest. Note the bird-houses at various points along the route.

3. Ignore a trail on the right as you pass a small concrete structure, and continue ahead to the top of a high bank where the route swings rightward toward the shore, now visible through the trees. Though the route here is easy

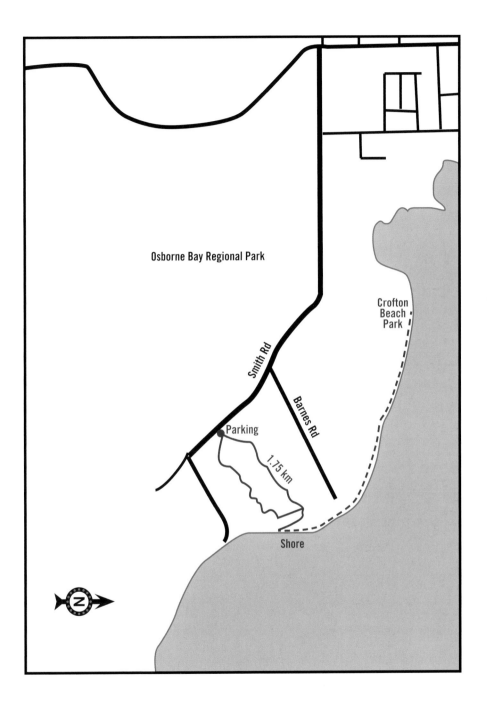

Osborne Bay Regional Park

Crofton Beach Park

Smith Rd

Barnes Rd

Parking

1.75 km

Shore

N

to descend, ascending it can be a bit of an exertion for those who aren't in particularly good shape.

4. Toward the end of the trail, turn left down a set of sturdy concrete-and-soil steps to reach the shore.

5. The beach is best explored at or near low tide, since it is overhung with arbutus near the tide line. When the tide is at least partly out, it is easy to walk to the left around the point at least as far as the Crofton Beach Park, 1.5 km distant. After exploring the beach, climb back up the trail via either the steps or the southern end of the trail a few dozen metres along the shore.

6. At the top of the bank, turn left onto either of two fairly constricted trails running parallel to the shore. Although narrow and possibly overhung with salal for the first few metres, these two tracks open out once under the cover of the tall cedars and firs and merge with each other. Occasional blazes of white spray paint on trees confirm that you're on the right trail.

7. Avoiding side tracks leading off to the summer camp visible through the trees at a few spots, return to the end of the trail near the road. Pass through a gap in the fence and return to your car along a broad, newly graded gravel strip.

RIGHT *The trail slopes significantly down the high bank but is well maintained and smooth.* (3)

LEFT *The beach is mostly fine gravel at low tide. At high tide it is best for swimming but can be shady in the afternoon. The north end of Salt Spring Island is directly across. (5)*

BELOW *The trail begins by crossing a large, open field with some lovely blossom trees and a large patch of (invasive, but tasty) Himalayan blackberries. (1)*

19. LADYSMITH MARINE WALK

Tucked into a wooded bank between the town of Ladysmith and its harbour, the walk covers various interconnected trails while passing several points of historical significance.

2.3-km loop	Easy
Starting and ending elevation: sea level High point: 18 m	All seasons

Difficulty: Most of the route is a broad, even, well-maintained path involving only a little change of altitude. The shorewalking section is along fine, smooth pebbles that are generally not slippery even in wet weather.

Start: From Highway 1 as it passes along the southeastern edge of Ladysmith, turn off at the traffic lights where you see a sign for Transfer Beach Park. Follow Transfer Beach Boulevard into the park to either the large parking lot to the left of the end of the road, by the amphitheatre, or the well-developed beach parking area near the washrooms to the right.

1. Retrace your steps along the paved road a short distance until you see a vertical post with a blue top and a trailhead marked "Marine Walk" (occasionally a little obscured by blackberry bushes). The first section of the trail winds along the top of a fairly high bank beneath mostly alder, maple and arbutus.

2. When you emerge onto a bit of old paved road, note the next blue-topped signpost straight ahead. Ignore for now the short section of abandoned road leading downhill to your right, though later this will be part of your return route. Cross to the next section of trail, now a

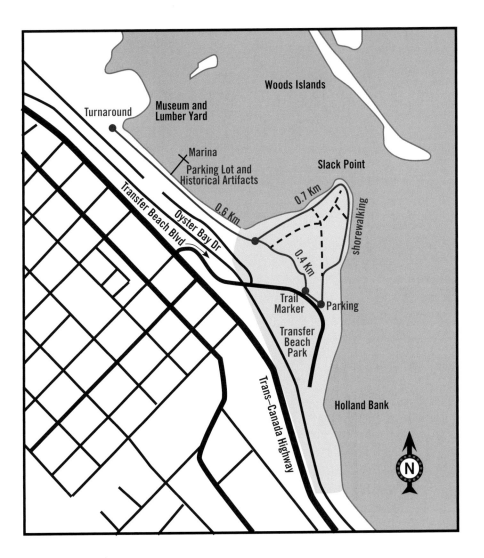

broad, even track of crushed gravel with a chain railing along one side. As you descend you will get glimpses of the harbour through the boughs of maples.

3. This section of trail ends in a parking area with some items of historical and natural interest. Apart from information on the purple martin recovery program, you will see a former navigational buoy, a "boom boat" and, straight ahead, abandoned railway lines. Now

a "rails to trails" conversion, these tracks run through small firs and maples just above the shore.

4. This section ends with two sets of stairs, one leading down to a marina (with toilet facilities and a floating café), the other up to the historic town of Ladysmith. For the recommended walk, however, turn back here and retrace your route along the previous two sections of trail. When you have climbed back up to the trail-head, with the abandoned road leading downhill, turn left. Two large blocking stones have been splashed with blue paint.

5. This part of the route follows a largely disintegrated asphalt road down to the historically fascinating "Slack Point," a reminder of the days, now long past, when Ladysmith was a busy harbour for coal. The coal was mined at Extension, 22 km north, and washed here with water piped from Holland Creek before shipping. Vast quantities of waste coal, or slack, built up into what is now a significant promontory. Slack Point (or "Slag Point" as it is sometimes called, inaccurately, even by place-name authorities such as GeoBC and the Atlas of Canada) is not currently park land, but its criss-crossing tracks through low bushes are much used by local dog walkers.

6. For the best route, do as most locals do and cut down toward the shore, composed of black fragments of coal waste. Follow the shore around the point for the best views across Ladysmith Harbour to the interesting sandstone Woods Island only 200 m away. Via a short section of wide, clear, user-made trail, make your back to the parking lot and Transfer Beach Park.

ABOVE *The interesting boats in the little harbour include a working fleet of trollers. (3)*

LEFT *The first part of the walk follows a ridge with some lovely old arbutus. (1)*

20. ROBERTS MEMORIAL PROVINCIAL PARK

An easy trail curving gently downward through firs, cedars and swordferns to a low grassy bluff along a shore of smooth, sculpted sandstone. Expect patches of wildflowers in the spring.

1.6 km return	Easy
Starting elevation: 30 m	All seasons

Start: Yellow Point Road is a long loop route that can be approached from either its northern end at Nanaimo or, more directly, from its southern end near Ladysmith. For the southern approach, 6 km north of Ladysmith, turn off the highway at traffic lights onto Cedar Road. After 2.8 km turn right onto Yellow Point Road. The park, about 9 km along, is well signposted from either direction. An ample parking lot lies almost immediately off the road.

Difficulty: The trail is generally broad and even, with only a few muddy spots or roots. The smooth sandstone shore provides good traction unless it is covered with algae, as it can be in winter or early spring.

1. The trail to the shore could hardly be more straightforward, since there are no significant side trails. Go directly ahead past the outhouse and begin a gently curving, gradual descent along a dirt path, mostly free of mud even in winter. The forest here is second growth, but many of the firs and cedars are large enough to be stately and the undergrowth of salal and swordferns is attractive.

2. As it approaches the shore the trail swings right and runs

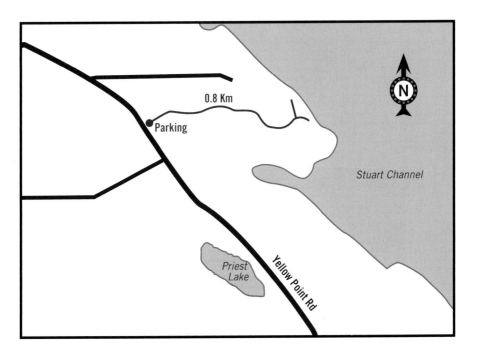

along a low, rounded ridge of sandstone. This section is geologically interesting because it is a miniature sample of the tilted sandstone ridges, running northwest–southeast, that constitute the peninsulas, bays and outcroppings of the bulk of the southern Gulf Islands.

3. As the trail swings toward the shore again and levels out, the trees thin. Here, in the mossy meadows, you can find some beautiful patches of spring wildflowers, especially fawn lilies. You will also see an outhouse a short distance off the main trail. With the shore in sight, you will find a cross trail and one going directly ahead. Since the foreshore area in the park is fairly small, you can wander at will without worrying about getting disoriented. In order to make a satisfying circuit, you may wish to head left at the first intersection until you reach the shore. From there, turn to your right and walk along the shoreline to the east end of the park, where the shore rises to small cliffs and the rock forms become more rugged.

Keep your eye out for a (very modern but attractive) "petroglyph."

4. Loop back to join the main shore trail and return the way you came.

ABOVE *The modern "petroglyph" near the southern end of the park. (3)*

RIGHT *The shore along the southern boundary of the park rises to small bluffs. It is easy to walk along either the trail or the top of the bluffs. (3)*

21. CABLE BAY TRAIL

Forests and ferns, shoreline trails along a sandstone bank through arbutus, views of Gabriola Island cliffs and the turbulent currents of the infamous Dodd Narrows.

Distance: 4.7 km return	Easy to moderate
Starting elevation: 85 m Low point: sea level	All seasons but a few muddy patches in winter or wet weather

Difficulty: Most of the trail to Cable Bay itself is broad and well graded, with switchbacks to reduce steep sections. The shoreline part of the trail (not in the park) is a little rough underfoot. Walking along the shore itself can require a little care to avoid slipping.

Start: From the junction where Highway 19A splits from Highway 19 south of Nanaimo, follow the signs to Cedar. By the Esso service station turn onto Holden Corso Road, and after 1.9 km take a slight left onto Barnes Road (the main through road). At 3.4 km turn left and drive 500 m along Nicola Road to its end in a large parking area with several signs.

Unfortunately, a controversial golf course and housing development are planned for the current forested area on either side of the path, but the intention is to leave the trail usable.

1. From the end of the parking lot and the signposted trailhead, follow the broad dirt track into a large stand of trees until it crosses under some power lines.

2. The trail passes through several sets of metal structures designed to prevent motorized vehicles from entering. Follow the trail as it crosses a private road, then a small bridge, and begins to descend. Cross a construction road. Just before the switchbacks a broad track leaves

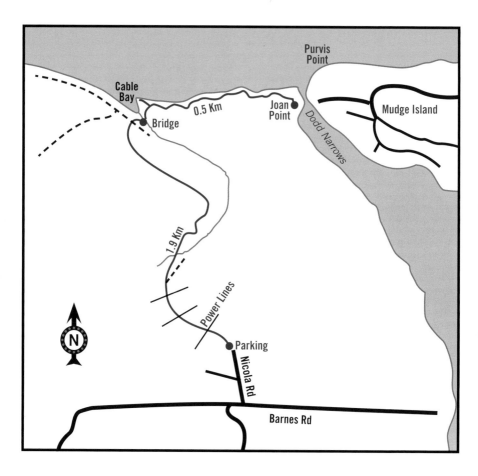

the trail on the right, but a signpost indicates Cable Bay Trail to be to the left.

3. Once you reach Cable Bay, about 1.6 km from the trail-head, you can take a small side path down onto the sand-stone ledges of this small, narrow, steep-sided bay.

4. You will see signs posted by a sturdy footbridge over the stream that flows into the bay, announcing this to be the park boundary but not prohibiting use of the bridge and continuing on the broad trails on the other side.

5. Once across the bridge, follow the track across the treed ridge and turn left to follow the trail a short distance

ABOVE *The sandstone cliffs of Gabriola Island. (5)*

BELOW *Boats often take advantage of slack current in Dodd Narrows. Mudge Island is directly across. (6)*

to a rounded meadow and an excellent viewpoint down Stuart Channel and across to the cliffs of Gabriola Island.

6. Turn back to rejoin the trail from the bridge and carry on straight ahead, parallel to the shore. This 1-km trail to Joan Point Park at Dodd Narrows is comparatively rough, requiring a little care stepping over roots and rocks. You can, if you prefer, walk most of the way along the largely sandstone shore, especially if the tide is out. If you arrive at the narrows when the current is at its strongest, and especially if it is ebbing, the sight across the turbulent waters to Mudge Island can be spectacular.

7. Return the way you came. (From the end of the shoreline trail by the narrows, you will see a well-established and attractive trail heading inland, but don't expect it to loop back: after 250 m it leads to a dirt construction road.)

One of many grand old maples, this one by the intersection between the trail and a gravel service road. (2)

22. JACK POINT AND BIGGS PARK

Garry oak and arbutus meadows, views of Nanaimo Harbour and coast mountains on one side, Protection and Gabriola islands on the other, and shoreline trails past bizarrely sculpted sandstone formations.

5 km return	Easy
Starting elevation: near sea level High point: 20 m	All seasons

Start: Turn off Highway 1 south of Nanaimo at the overpass for the Duke Point ferries. Turn right onto MacMillan Road, also signposted with the park's name. Once on Maughan Road, about 3.5 km from the highway, turn right onto Jackson Road, again signposted for the park. Follow the road to the signposted parking lot.

Difficulty: A well-graded and well-engineered path with even surfaces. Three large wooden staircases eliminate chances of slipping at what would otherwise be steep sections of trail.

1. Walk under the highway through the pedestrian tunnel and turn right to follow the broad, even, level path parallel to the highway. Before long a tall evergreen hedge largely buffers the effects of the passing cars en route to the Duke Point ferry terminal.

2. You will soon reach a boardwalk and stairs, the first of three sets between here and the point. A curious feature is that on your outward trip all of the staircases have you climbing, but you nevertheless end up at sea level.

3. When you reach an irregularity in the shoreline with a small, treed peninsula forming a bay, consider leaving

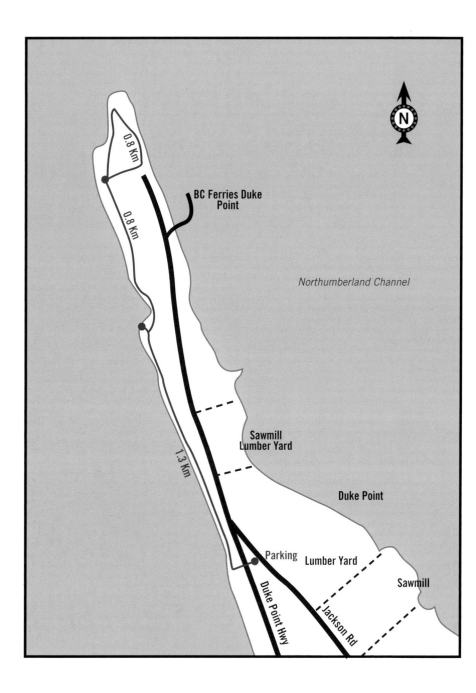

N

0.8 Km

0.8 Km

BC Ferries Duke
Point

Northumberland Channel

1.3 Km

Sawmill
Lumber Yard

Duke Point

Parking   Lumber Yard

Sawmill

Duke Point Hwy

Jackson Rd

the trail to explore the strange sandstone rock formations characteristic of the whole peninsula but particularly easy to reach here. Return to the trail.

4. When you come to the base of the largest set of stairs, again leave the trail, this time to look for the Aboriginal "petroglyph," resembling salmon, on a large boulder on the shore, facing out to sea.

5. Near the tip of the long, narrow peninsula, you will come to a junction. Since the trail forms a loop, you can go in either direction, but it is recommended that you keep straight ahead and, after rounding the tip of the peninsula, walk along the low, shelving sandstone by the water's edge before rejoining the trail to begin your return journey. From this point, you are close to the Duke Point ferry terminal. Some will be fascinated by watching the ferry traffic; others not. Also from this return part of the loop, you will have views of the cliffs of Gabriola and the small ferry running continuously to and from the island.

6. The trail recrosses the tip of the narrow peninsula and links back onto the main trail to the starting point.

Weathered Douglas fir and a section of boardwalk shortly before the loop trail cuts across the tip of the point. (5)

ABOVE *It is worthwhile leaving the path to explore the nooks and crannies of this little peninsula, midway along the south shore. (3)*

BELOW *This intriguingly sculpted area of sandstone lies below the trail just beyond the little peninsula. (3)*

23. NEWCASTLE ISLAND MARINE PROVINCIAL PARK

A perimeter walk around a forested island with warm, sandy beaches, seaside meadows, clifftop views from old-growth forest, striking sandstone formations, and historic and cultural sites.

Distance: 8.5 km (shortcuts possible)	Easy to moderate (but quite long)
Starting elevation: sea level High point: 45 m	Mid-spring to early autumn (when the ferry is running)

Start: From Highway 1 through the centre of Nanaimo, turn toward the harbour down Comox Road immediately south of Pearson Bridge. After 100 m turn in to Maffeo Sutton Park parking lot. Walk toward the northeast shore of the park, following the signs to "Newcastle Ferry." Ferries run more or less continuously all day during the summer. The crossing is 1 km and takes about 20 minutes.

Difficulty: The trails are wide and for the most part level and well groomed. The walking is easy, with no steep hills and little elevation change. Because of the the trail's considerable length, though, some may rate it "moderate" rather than "easy." Beachwalking is also generally easy, but be careful stepping along or over logs and seaweed.

1. Walk straight ahead either on the broad footpath through the grassy area or along the shoreline. The "pavilion" on the forest side of the grassy area was used as a dance hall for cruise ships from Vancouver in the 1930s and 40s. Today you'll find a concession stand there. Brownie Bay, the first inlet you come to, has a sandy beach at low tide

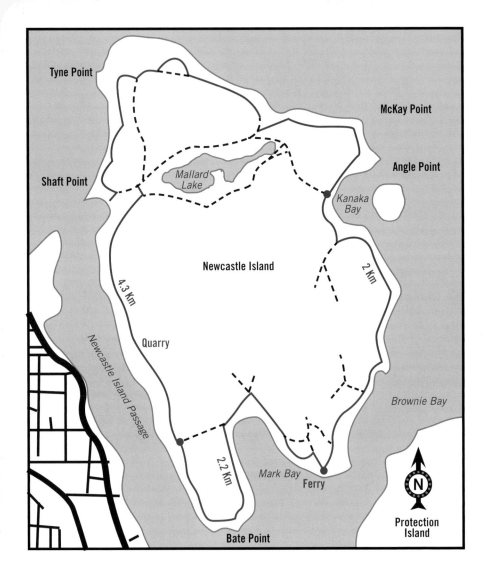

and is probably the best swimming beach on the island. It dries completely at very low tides, making it possible to walk all the way across to Protection Island.

2. Rejoin the shoreline trail or walk along the sandstone shore all the way to Kanaka Bay. Here you will find outhouses and a junction with a path cutting across the island. Cyclists, who have been sharing the path with

ABOVE *The quarry still has jumbled chunks of stone, some of them clearly intended to be used as millstones. (4)*

BELOW *The upper beach of Brownie Bay with its fine, white sand is particularly good for sunbathing. The trail through the meadows here is especially easy. (1)*

walkers until this point, must use this optional, inland path.

3. As you walk north from Kanaka Bay, you will have to use the shoreline trail, as the shore itself is narrow and increasingly irregular. The trail climbs gradually through some magnificent old firs past Angle Point and McKay Point until you reach Giovando Lookout, about 45 m above sea level. The rock formations on the cliffs below are particularly striking along this stretch of coast. About two-thirds of the way along this section, a path to the left leads a short distance inland to Mallard Lake. You may wish to take a peek at the lake before returning to the much more scenic coast trail. An outhouse is located a short distance from here near the continuation of the shoreline trail and a second trail junction to Mallard Lake.

4. Rounding the tip of the island and passing Tyne Point, you will find that your view has changed to one of Nanaimo. As the trail drops you will come to a sequence of pebbly beaches. You may wish to leave the trail to explore these. There is another set of outhouses just inland from the southernmost of them. You may also want to explore the sandstone shore (see photograph) before returning to the Channel Trail. In a short distance you will come to an historic quarry where sandstone was removed for millstones and architectural features for such distant destinations as San Francisco.

5. From the quarry, the trail leads through forest to a junction. You can shorten the overall distance by about 1 km by cutting the 400 m across the base of Bate Point rather than walking the full coast trail.

6. The route back to the ferry ends in a grassy area above the boat docks. Make sure you arrive in plenty of time before the last ferry.

24. PIPERS LAGOON PARK

A varied walk around a strikingly convoluted piece of shoreline, through forest, along a sandy beach and over several headlands. Excellent views of the picturesque "Shack Island" and passing BC Ferries.

2.4 km return	Easy to moderate
High point: 34 m Low point: sea level	All seasons

Start: From Highway 19A through Nanaimo, turn right when you see the sign for BC Ferries Departure Bay and, almost immediately, at the next traffic light, left onto Departure Bay Road. After 1.9 km turn right onto Hammond Bay Road and continue for 2.6 km until you see a small, dead-end road on your right called Chinook Road. Because parking is possible for only a few cars on the shoulder, you may have to continue downhill to Lagoon Road and then turn right onto Place Road to park in the main lot. If at all possible, though, opt for the Chinook Road start, since this short trail through the forest is an attractive beginning to the walk.

Difficulty: Most of the route is very easy, but you will need sturdy shoes and some agility to clamber over the rocky bump separating the isthmus from the rest of the quasi-island. The beach logs can be slippery when wet.

1. From Chinook Road, enter the tunnel-like trail in the heavy vegetation by the signpost saying "Beach Access" and descend through the forest down a stepped path. You will soon be by the parking lot for Pipers Lagoon Park, the alternative beginning of the walking route.

2. Cross the grassy field to the right and climb over the logs

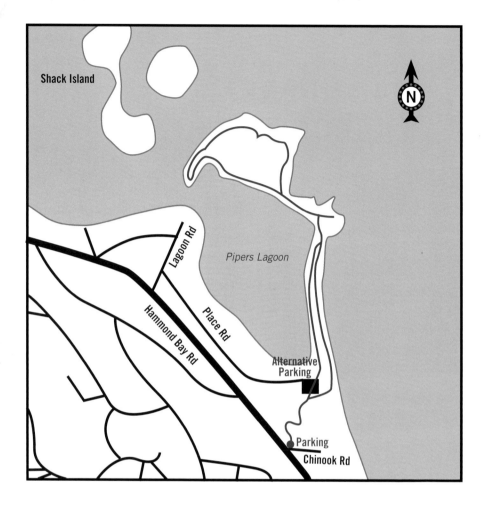

to the beach. Walk along the upper beach of the narrow isthmus from its pebbly south end to the sandy north end and climb over the logs onto the wide, level path.

3. Follow the path onto the rocky headland, turning right to explore the smaller headland at the east end of the rocky area. Return to the main route to the rest of the rocky quasi-island and scramble up and over the rocky outcropping that blocks the way.

4. Walk along the path, following the log-strewn upper

ABOVE *After passing over a rocky outcropping, the trail along the wooded peninsula broadens out. (4)*

BELOW *The eastern end of the outer beach is especially sandy at low tide. (2)*

shoreline of two short, pebbly beaches separated by a small, rocky headland.

5. Climb onto the exposed grassy headland and follow the path through the sparse fir and Garry oak forest above the northeast-facing rocky beach until you come to the tip of the headland with great views of Shack Island. In winter, sea lions can be seen rolling past the shore.

6. Follow the path along the top of the low, rocky cliffs until you come to the curious grassy spit that nearly cuts off the entrance to Pipers Lagoon (called "Pages Lagoon" on some maps). Leave the path at this point and explore the spit by walking along its shoreline. The views across Hammond Bay on the one side and the lagoon and head-land on the other are wonderful.

7. Climb back up to rejoin the shoreside path that runs along the north side of the lagoon until you reconnect with the trail you used to circle the promontory. The lagoon itself is an excellent spot (at or near high tide) to view great blue herons and other waterfowl.

8. Follow the main path up and over the rocky outcropping and then along the top of the spit back to the parking area.

9. Return the way you came.

25. NECK POINT PARK

Rocky headlands with several pebble beaches, boardwalks, spring flowers and forest trails. Great views of Hammond Bay, Shack Island and Pipers Lagoon.

2.4 km loop	Easy
Starting elevation: 13 m High point: 23 m	All seasons

Start: On the northern outskirts of Nanaimo, by the Brooks Landing Shopping Mall on Highway 1A, turn north at the traffic lights and a large sign for BC Ferries. Almost immediately, take the first left onto Departure Bay Road. After 1.9 km, turn right onto Hammond Bay Road for 4.9 km. Turn right onto McGuffie Road for 400 m and bear right to the end of Keel Cove Lane. Please note that the main, signposted entrance and parking lot for the park are off Hammond Bay Road, 600 m farther back, on Morningstar Road. The starting point recommended here has very limited parking but makes for the most satisfying loop walk.

Difficulty: Except for the need to climb some steps, the path is suitable even for those with walking difficulties. Leaving the path to explore some of the headlands, as recommended, requires securing footing on potentially slippery logs and rocks.

1. The first section of the trail involves climbing up a wooden staircase (with handrail) to a superb high viewpoint over Sunset Beach at the northwest side of the peninsula. As you go down the staircases and approach the beach, ignore side trails to the right and walk to the end of the beach.

2. Follow the broad trail inland away from the beach until

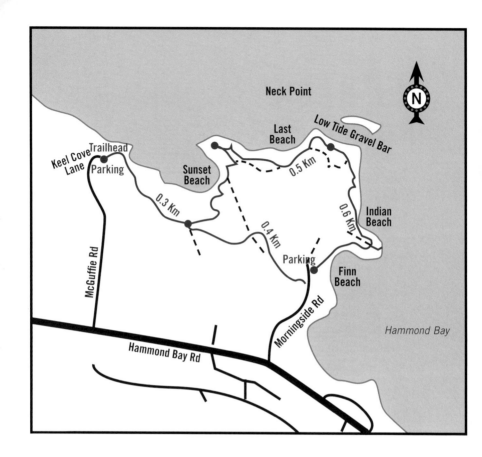

you see another trail leading sharply to the left. Take this trail as it climbs onto a headland and leads to an excellent viewpoint. Besides the usual year-round wildlife – bald eagles, harbour seals, cormorants – sea lions can be spotted from Neck Point from autumn to spring.

3. Return along the first 100 m of this trail, but then take the first fork to the left to follow the clifftop before being joined by another trail merging from the right. Ignore the next right-hand trail and descend to Last Beach, where you will find a picnic table.

4. At the north end of this beach, climb up more steps to continue along the rock bluffs of the north end of Neck Point itself. It is worthwhile at this point to leave the

ABOVE *The boardwalk near the easternmost part of the peninsula is especially elaborate. (4)*

BELOW *The beach tucked inside Hammond Bay with a good view of Shack Island and, beyond, the headland outside Pipers Lagoon. (5)*

trail and walk along the crest of the striking gravel bar leading out to a small rocky outcropping.

5. Returning to the blufftop trail, climb over another bump via more stairs and boardwalk and descend to walk along the upper shore of Indian Beach. Although the old, established trail cuts inland, carry on along the top of the beach to walk out onto the easternmost headland, a recently acquired addition to the park. Here you will find curious concrete structures and metal railings, the remnants of a private dwelling and its facilities. The small, irregular buildings on the picturesque islet in the middle of Hammond Bay are summer cabins on Shack Island. In the 1930s these odd little cottages were the base of local fishermen.

6. Join the clear path circling this last headland before descending to Finn Beach, the last one, beside the main park entrance. Cross the parking area and walk a little way along the paved road until you come to a wide, level path (signposted "Annie Clark's Way") cutting to the right, back across the base of the whole headland. When you come to a fork to the left, leave this broad trail for a smaller one climbing upward to the left. Rejoin the path by which you first entered the park and return to your vehicle.

26. MOORECROFT REGIONAL PARK

A lagoon-like cove that drains at low tide and forest walks to rocky headlands with picnic tables, weather-beaten trees and island-studded views. Several trails through a forest of large firs and cedars.

2.4-km loop	Easy
Elevation changes negligible	All seasons

Start: From Highway 19 between Parksville and Nanaimo, turn onto Northwest Bay Road at the Nanoose Bay Petro-Canada station (traffic lights). After 3 km, turn right onto Stewart Road. Follow it 2.7 km to its end, at Moorecroft Regional Park.

Difficulty: Since the former summer camp became a regional park in 2011, a lot of work has gone into installing raised path beds of crushed gravel, and at one spot a sturdy boardwalk, over sections of the broad trails that were always muddy in winter. On the whole the walking is extremely easy except possibly on the rocky shore.

1. Follow the broad track toward the bay. Climb the slight rise on your right as you approach the water and follow the narrow path below an old building (one of the few remnants of the former church camp) out onto the small breakwater-like promontory called Cooks Point.

2. Retrace your route to join the main path. Follow it around the base of Arab Cove (unsignposted) to Vesper Point, ignoring signs to the "meadow" on your left. You will pass a short gravel loop path that rejoins the main trail after a few dozen metres. A set of wooden stairs on your right leads up to a picnic table on a grassy hill with lovely views.

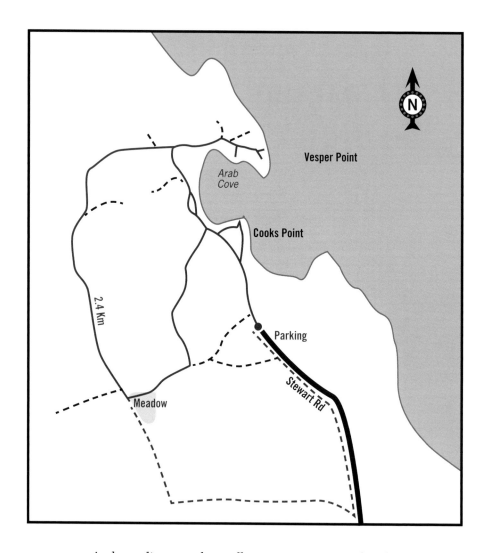

A short distance along allows you access to the shore, though swimming is possible only at or near high tide. As you round the cove, ignore two more signposts to the left to the "Meadow" and head instead toward "Vesper Point." Later you will pass a broad unsignposted track to your left. Ignore this, as well, since it leads to a section of the forest bristling with "No Trespassing" signs.

3. As you approach the rocky point on the ocean side of

the cove, you will find a small network of trails with bizarrely oversized split-cedar fences designed to keep you on the trails and prevent you from stomping on natural habitat. The first branch to the right leads to a lovely grassy meadow with picnic tables. The main route leads to a higher, rocky area with weathered firs and Garry oaks. The pair of islands 5 km offshore are the Ballenas Islands. The close island, 1 km away, is Gerald Island, now a provincial park. Many other islands – Yeo, Amelia, Winchelseas – dot the view southeast toward Nanaimo.

4. Return to the base of the cove to pick up the signposted trail to the "Meadow." This broad track leads gradually uphill through beautifully forested land. Although the trees are hardly ancient, the maples, firs and cedars, interspersed with glades of sword and lady ferns, are extremely attractive. Ignore a small but clear trail to the right, since it leads to private land where vehement signs will turn you back. Also ignore a broad track on your left signposted for the "Beach." This leads back to the base of the cove.

5. When you reach a kind of T-junction, turn left toward the meadow. A level, well-maintained trail to the right at this T-junction leads to a subdivision off Dorcas Point Road (an alternative starting point for a visit to the park). Walk along the edge of the grassy area, formerly a playing field for the church camp.

6. At the end of the meadow, turn left to pick up another broad track that leads back to the main trail near the parking lot. Although you could walk straight ahead to go directly to the parking area, you can also extend your whole walk and see more of the forest by taking the first of two broad trails to the left. This will take you back to Arab Cove and from there back to your vehicle.

OPTION

From the end of the meadow, instead of turning left, you can continue straight ahead onto a new gravel trail that leads out of the park to a land allowance. Turn left onto a clear but small trail past an open area with newly planted firs. You will emerge onto Stewart Road a few hundred metres from the parking lot. Since the road is so quiet, it makes for a pleasant walk back to your vehicle (an additional 1 km).

OPPOSITE *A zoom in on Mt. Diadem, one of several jagged peaks across the Strait of Georgia. (3)*

LEFT *A typical section of forest along the well-groomed trails. (4)*

BELOW *The picnic site near Vesper Point. (3)*

27. RATHTREVOR PROVINCIAL PARK

A popular spot with local walking groups. A broad, level path almost entirely near the seashore, partly through mature fir forest, partly through open meadows with picnic tables. Easy access to a vast, low-tide beach of sand and tide pools.

4 km return (plus beachwalking)	Easy
Elevation throughout: sea level	All seasons

Start: Most visitors to the park use the main, signposted entrance directly off Highway 19A south of Parksville. The recommended starting point here, though little used, does allow the best continuous walking route. From Highway 19A just south of the bridge over Englishman River at the south end of Parksville, turn onto Plummer Road. After 1.2 km turn slightly right, onto Shorewood Drive until it curves sharply to the right. After 1 km, at the end of Shorewood and the beginning of Rico's Lane, park outside the gates for this end of Rathtrevor Park.

Difficulty: This could hardly be an easier trail. Level, smooth and wide, it also passes several benches and rest stops. If you choose to walk part of the route on the beach, however, be a little careful if the logs are wet.

1. The first part of the trail, through mature Douglas fir forest (some of it with woodpecker holes), is more or less close to the shore and only slightly above it. Several trails to the right lead to the provincial park campground tucked completely out of sight amidst the trees. On the sea side of the trail, continual erosion from winter storms requires occasional rerouting of the trails farther away from the shore. Several short trails lead to

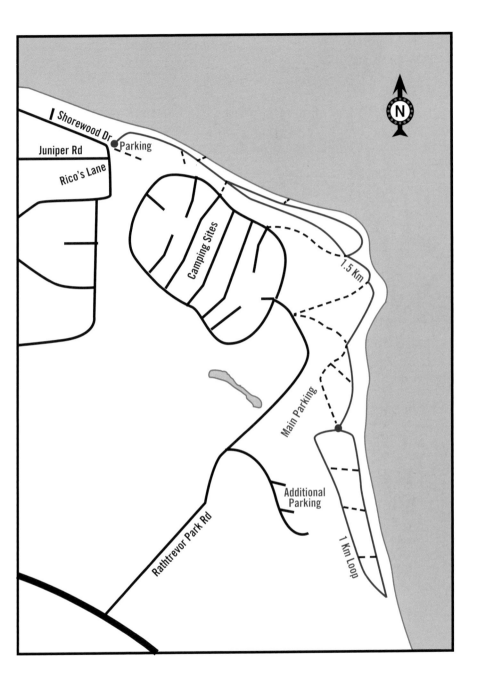

Shorewood Dr

Juniper Rd

Rico's Lane

Parking

Camping Sites

1.5 Km

Main Parking

Additional Parking

Rathtrevor Park Rd

1 Km Loop

N

the shore. Low, split-cedar fences line much of this first section. As the track passes the campground and more options to a network of trails appear, keep left to enjoy the proximity of the ocean.

2. Leaving the forest, the trail crosses a broad open area of stunted and weathered firs, sea meadows and picnic facilities. Flowering currant, wild roses, woolly sunflowers and sea grass are common in this section. Take time to look at the interpretive signs. The closest island, 3 km away, is the oddly named Mistaken Island. Behind that, the twin Ballenas Islands are visible, along with the most spectacular of the Coast Mountains, Mt. Tantalus, with its unmistakable year-round snowfields and glaciers.

3. The third phase of the route is actually an old roadbed dating from the time, decades ago, when the whole waterfront area under the trees ahead was part of a privately run campsite. Now a picnic area, this grassy section of the park is dotted with firs. The beach in front of this section of the route is the sandiest and most extensive.

4. After reaching the end of the park, clearly evident because a continuous development of resorts and condominiums begins here, turn back and retrace your steps to the edge of the forest.

5. When you reach the edge of the woods, take the path that angles slightly into the trees. Ignore the various side trails crossing this track, since the route straight ahead runs parallel to the shore and will deliver you back to your starting point. Although you will catch occasional glimpses of tents or people in the nearby camping area, this trail is worth walking because it passes many of the largest firs.

OPTION

In warm weather and when the tide is out, you may wish to include a large circuit of the vast area of sandy shore, extending nearly 700 m to the low-tide mark.

LEFT Wild rose bushes and weathered split-cedar fences are characteristic features of the second section of the route. (2)

BELOW The south Ballenas Island with the mountains over Howe Sound in the background. (2)

28. ALBERNI INLET TRAIL

The first phase of a planned long-distance coastline trail rising and falling over the sunny, rocky bluffs and richly varied terrain of the inlet's eastern shore. In general, the farther south, the more attractive the trail.

24 km return (feels much longer); one-way shuttle possible	Moderate but long
Starting elevation: 140 m High point: 290 m Height gain: 300 m over many rises and drops	All seasons

Start: Entering Port Alberni, take the left fork toward Bamfield. After 3.8 km, turn left onto 10th Avenue at the traffic lights. Drive 1.2 km and turn left onto Argyle Street for 300 m. Turn right onto Anderson Avenue, signposted for Bamfield. After 2.2 km, at a T-junction you will see the large, new sign and parking lot for the Alberni Inlet Trail.

Difficulty: The trail has been carefully prepared with a good surface where possible, plus switchbacks, earth-and-timber stairs and so on. A few stretches are nevertheless quite steep and rough, with some loose dirt underfoot. From early July through September, some parts of the trail, especially in the centre section, are deep in slippery, freshly fallen arbutus leaves. Sturdy day hikers or boots with a good grip help considerably.

1. The broad, easy trail begins by ascending gradually through second-growth firs with the occasional large "wolf tree." Partway up, pass a smaller trail forking right (though it rejoins soon after). As the trail levels out and contours to the right, views of distant Strathcona Park peaks, over the city and toward Mt. Arrowsmith, open impressively (best in the spring).

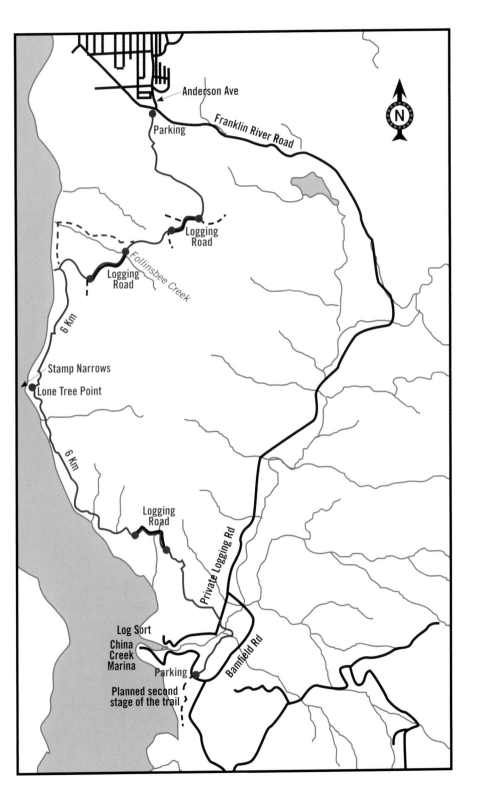

2. Turn right onto a logging road through a fresh clear-cut, and after a few minutes enter the small, second-growth woods on a clearly signposted path. The largely level trail brings you closer to the inlet and, after a bridge, a split. Those who prefer the easier route can opt for the right fork, parallel to Follinsbee Creek. The more interesting alternative is to go left, although it begins with an uninspiring tromp along logging roads. Ignoring two smaller side roads, follow the flagged through road until you come to an open area with a pleasant view over the head of the inlet and the Somass River estuary. The drop to the shore from here is quite steep. Except for a short section along a ridge, though, it isn't vertiginous or difficult. In fact, there are some sections in the middle part of the "moderate" trail that are virtually as steep as this officially "difficult" section.

3. Dropping toward the shore and larger trees, switchback upward a little, then descend to walk parallel to the shore with glimpses of log booms through the trees. Come to a sea-level promontory with a lovely little rocky beach and signs of an improvised campsite. This is the most popular destination and turnaround spot, but those who turn around here miss the more beautiful trail farther south.

4. The trail next runs parallel to and above the shore, which usually is lined with log booms. Take the time to leave the trail and visit a rocky shorefront promontory that features a large fir. An even better viewpoint comes a little farther along, at a sunny open area of grassy and rocky outcropping with a navigation light. At this point, Stamp Narrows, the inlet is barely 500 m wide, so this is an excellent spot for watching boats of all shapes and sizes. This is close to the midpoint of the trail.

5. Walk close to the shore first, then climb up a fairly steep

LEFT *Deep green pools in the bridged creek running by the last section of trail before the parking spot. (8)*

BELOW *The rocky promontory at Lone Tree Point at Stamp Narrows, looking north. (4)*

section, first past arbutus and then along the base of some picturesquely mossy cliffs. The trail climbs steadily to about 100 m above the shore, culminating in some bluffs with good views and dotted with beautiful little manzanita.

6. Drop fairly steeply to the shore and pass a small, rough beach that is pleasant enough for a rest, though it is surrounded by a log breakwater and looks north to a busy log-sorting site. Turning inland, the trail becomes wide, easy and beautifully maintained, passing a few old-growth giants as it climbs. You emerge from the forest into a clear-cut and a logging road. Although the ascent along this road to over 200 m can be baking hot, it does provide increasingly splendid views far down the inlet.

7. As the road approaches some small trees, look for a small trailhead and posted map. This phase of the trail is unlike any previous one. It curves and twists over a descending series of open mossy knolls dotted with small lodgepole pines. The final few hundred metres leading to a busy logging road can be weedy in early summer.

8. Cross the logging road and enter the forest at a sign-posted trailhead. This last section is possibly the most beautiful of the entire trail. Two metal bridges lead over a crystal-clear stream to a trail running parallel to a small gorge surrounded by a deep forest of large hemlock and cedar. When you come out onto a paved road, counter-intuitively turn left to reach the small parking area near a set of gates. If you are hitchhiking back to your vehicle, walk a short distance past this to the Bamfield road and turn left. Otherwise, return the way you came. Be aware that the road to your right leads to China Creek marina, possibly relevant in your long-distance planning. (There is a campground and RV site by the marina.)

29. WILD PACIFIC TRAIL

The only day-use trail on Vancouver Island that runs next to a rugged shore fully exposed (in sections) to the open Pacific Ocean. The trail includes protected coves with beach access, a lighthouse, unusual vegetation and several rest stops.

17 km return (with shorter options)	Easy
Elevation throughout: near sea level	All seasons

Start: From the Pacific Rim National Park visitor centre, located at the T-junction with Highway 4, turn left to Ucluelet. Upon entering Ucluelet, drive through the town along Peninsula Road until, just before its end, you come to an intersection with Coast Guard Drive. Turn right and follow the signs to the signposted parking lot for the Wild Pacific Trail.

Difficulty: The trail is well graded, wide and has a generally even surface. The only difficulties may be encountered by those who leave the trail to gain access to the rocky shore. Slippery, uneven surfaces and exposure to rogue waves when seas are high require caution. Protected coves at Little Beach, Terrace Beach and Big Beach are the best places to explore the shore.

Directions are for the full trail currently connected via a 2-km section along residential streets. Some may thus prefer to walk the trail in two sections. Others may wish to arrange shuttle transportation in order to avoid repeating the trail on the return route. Kudos must go to the locals whose hard work and intrepid spirit created the trail.

1. From the Coast Guard Road parking lot, the trail heads directly to a protected rocky indentation of the coast. This first section of the trail, to Amphitrite Lighthouse, has the best views towards Barclay Sound and sunrises.

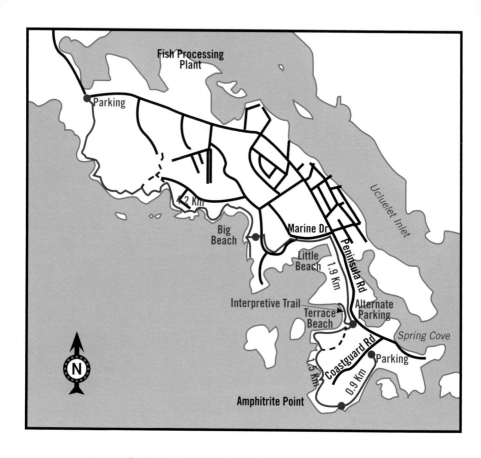

On the map: Fish Processing Plant, Parking, Ucluelet Inlet, 4.2 Km, Big Beach, Marine Dr, Little Beach, Peninsula Rd, 1.9 Km, Interpretive Trail, Terrace Beach, Alternate Parking, Spring Cove, Coastguard Rd, 1.5 Km, 0.9 Km, Parking, Amphitrite Point, N

2. From the lighthouse follow the main trail past a deeply inset cove, but take the time to visit two short viewpoint trails. Both lead to exposed promontories particularly thrilling when the waves are kicking up foam and fury. The loop concludes by entering He-Tin-Kis Park and the increasingly protected shore of Terrace Beach. When you first enter the park you will come to a fork in the trail. To follow the shore, keep left to pass picnic tables. For those who want to include a little beach walking in their visit to this trail, this is an easily-walked shore. Return to the main trail by walking along the new interpretive trail just above the shore, with interesting information on First Nations history.

ABOVE *Amphitrite Lighthouse is not huge but plays a crucial role along this dangerous section of coast. Fog and reefs have made this area a "graveyard of the Pacific" for shipwrecks. (1)*

BELOW *Terrace Beach makes a good side trip for those who want to leave the main trail and explore an intertidal zone. (2)*

3. To walk to the next section of currently developed trail, head down an old road leading to Peninsula Road and turn left onto Marine Drive until you see a trailhead leading directly towards the shore and some picnic tables by Big Beach.

4. After Big Beach, turn inland until you come to the access to Brown's Beach. Follow the zig--zagging trail above some especially rugged little coves. After a few hundred metres, the trail dips away from the shoreline to accommodate a road allowance before returning to the shore and, in a short distance, another exposed promontory.

5. From here you will have almost 3 km of uninterrupted walking, most of it close to the exposed shore or in sight of it through strikingly weathered trees. Near the beginning pass two trails leading to the Forbes Street parking and forest trail. Visit the new "Artists Loops" and storm watching platforms. The last part of the trail runs inland through interestingly deformed vegetation. Brightly coloured moss, bunchberries ("miniature dogwood") and deer ferns create beautiful natural gardens.

6. Unless you have arranged a shuttle to pick you up at the west trailhead along the highway entering Ucluelet, return to your starting point the way you came.

OPTIONS

To shorten your return journey you have several options:

1. Rejoin the trail via the Forbes Road access trail, in itself a beautiful bit of walking through interesting vegetation.

2. Walk through "downtown" Ucluelet along Peninsula Road, stopping for a little refreshment (or a lot).

3. Follow the trail the way you came until you come to the He-Tin-Kis trailhead. Instead of walking the circular route to your car, hike the 100 m along Peninsula Road.

30. HALFMOON BAY AND FLORENCIA BAY

A two-forked trail with each branch leading down dramatic staircases through old-growth forest to two separate inlets: first, tiny Halfmoon Bay with its beautiful sandy beach and rocky headlands, and then the south end of 5-km long Florencia Bay with its breaking surf.

Distance: 3.8 km return (plus beachwalking)	Easy
Starting elevation and high point: 40 m	All seasons (can be wet)

Start: From the Pacific Rim Park Tourist Information office (where you can get a parking pass), turn left toward Ucluelet. At almost exactly 2 km, look for the sign for Willowbrae Road on the right. Willowbrae is easy to miss because it looks like a suburban residential street. The only prominent sign is for the Wya Point Campground. Park at the end of Willowbrae, outside the campground gate and beside an outhouse.

Difficulty: With the exception of the Wild Pacific Trail by Ucluelet, this is the easiest day hike in this area. Most of the trail is a broad, level strip of crushed gravel. The descents to both bays do involve long sequences of wooden stairs and ramps, particularly twisting in the case of the one to Halfmoon Bay. In spite of the treads on the ramps, the wood can be slippery when wet.

1. The first part of the trail is an easy tromp down nearly level crushed gravel.

2. Turn left at the fork. This section of the trail is twisting and laced with roots. You will walk over sections of boardwalk, some of them heavily worn, and climb a few stairs. Several huge cedars line the trail.

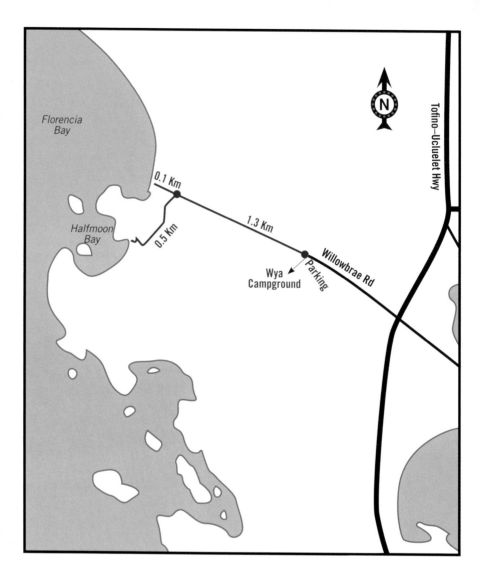

3. The last section of the trail leads through some giant
   Sitka spruce as you begin a complex series of treaded
   ramps and staircases twisting down the bank. Be particularly careful at the last bit of boardwalk. At the time of
   writing, it led into empty space, since it had been broken
   away by winter storms. You should have no difficulty
   picking your way down the last metre through logs and
   onto the sandy upper shore.

LEFT *A characteristically weathered and deformed red cedar along the Halfmoon side trail. (2)*

BELOW *The hard-packed sand of the bay makes for easy walking, especially at low tide. (4)*

4. Explore as much of the cove as you like, paying particular attention to the animal life on the rocks and tide pools at the north end of the cove. Climb back up the staircase and retrace the forested trail to the junction.

5. Turn left and go the short distance to the wooden staircase leading to the south end of Florencia Bay. These stairs are less twisty than the ones leading to Halfmoon Bay, requiring less care. Once you get to Florencia Bay you may feel tempted to walk the entire length of the beach. If you do, you can arrange a pickup at the other access near the end of the beach, accessible by road down the route to Wickaninnish Beach. During wet months, though, you will have to wade a stream in order to reach the other end of the beach. Florencia Bay gets its name from one of many shipwrecks along this stretch of coast.

An elaborate sequence of ramps and stairs leads to the shore. (3)

31. SOUTH BEACH AND NUU-CHAH-NULTH TRAIL

A striking boardwalk through a "garden" of bog-stunted pine and hemlock leading to two adjoining beaches. The first is a small cove with a beautiful curve of fine sand; the second is the south end of Wickaninnish Beach, part of the longest stretch of sand in the park and a favourite surfing spot.

5.2 km return (plus beachwalking)	Easy
Starting elevation: 15 m, drop to sea level and reascend to 15 m	All seasons

Start: After getting your day parking pass at the Pacific Rim National Park visitor centre, turn right where Highway 4 forms a T-junction with the road to Ucluelet. Go 4.7 km to the turn to Wickaninnish Beach, which some call Wick Road, and turn left. Drive down this road 1.4 km until you see the sign for Florencia Bay on your left. The parking lot is 1 km along.

Difficulty: The trail is mostly level, beginning with a little uneven footing over roots and requiring ducking under one log. In wet seasons, you will encounter a little mud. By far the largest section is on a long boardwalk with only a few occasional stairs. Vibram-soled shoes can be slippery on wet wood, and the trail can be a bit of a narrow squeeze when you meet others, but otherwise the walking could hardly be easier. Once the trail splits, each route to the two beaches involves a few stairs and some ramps, but with lots of anti-slip protection.

1. As a prelude to your walk, you may wish to go 100 m or so down the trail toward Florencia Bay, at least until you

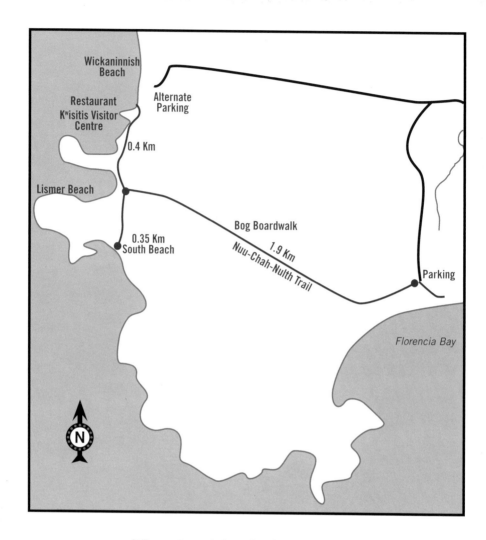

get a clifftop view of the 5-km long sweep of the beach and, usually, large surf.

2. Returning to the signposted trailhead and turning left, you will find yourself walking through some dramatically twisted and moss-hung old-growth trees, hemlock prominent amongst them. Watch your step over uneven roots, occasional muddy patches and the odd bit of boardwalk.

3. The second section is the most unusual feature of this

LEFT *The first part of trail has many interesting large trees. Here a hemlock became suspended after its nurse log rotted away.* (2)

BELOW
Looking back toward the trailhead from partway along South Beach. (5)

particular route. The boardwalk is nearly straight for over a kilometre, raised slightly above a bog full of interesting vegetation. Most striking are the trees. Stunted because they are growing in such wet conditions, the hemlock, the yellow cedar and especially the pines have oddly ornamental, "umbrella"-like shapes.

4. As the trail rises and then gradually descends, you will come to a lovely viewpoint onto a small strand between South Beach and Wickaninnish Beach. Locally this beach is named after artist Arthur Lismer, of Group of Seven fame, who spent many summers at a cabin here. Turn left onto the signposted trail to Second Beach and begin a descent over sections of steps and boardwalk past a few huge shorefront spruce.

5. The trail arrives on the beach at the head of a protected area of sand tucked behind headlands. You can begin your exploration of the cove by going in either direction, though the majority of the beach, as you will see, is to your left. Take care if the surf is high.

6. Return to the junction, and this time take the route toward Wickaninnish Beach. En route you can leave the main trail to get access to the small bay mentioned earlier called "Lismer Beach," separated from the main beach by a rock outcropping. Once on the main beach you can visit the beautifully arranged visitor centre, indulge yourself in the restaurant, watch surfers or, like most visitors arriving by car, head off for many kilometres down the long sweep of strand.

7. Unless you have arranged a shuttle, return to your starting point the way you came.

32. SCHOONER COVE

A fantasy-inspiring sequence of curving boardwalks, winding staircases and multi-level bridges through a stand of equally fantastical, mature trees. The trail leads to the extreme northwest end of the 15-km stretch of sand that starts with Wickaninnish Beach.

2 km return (plus beachwalking)	Easy
Starting elevation and high point: 23 m	All seasons

Start: Stop to buy your day parking pass at the Pacific Rim National Park visitor centre at the T-junction of Highway 4 with the road to Ucluelet. Turn right toward Tofino to stay on Highway 4. The Schooner Beach parking lot is signposted off the highway about 18 km along.

Difficulty: This complex system of boardwalks and staircases, many sections having handrails, is generally in very good condition. Since the otherwise muddy stretches are avoided, walking is on the whole easy and straightforward. In wet weather some parts are slippery, but most have good traction. The trail has occasionally been closed when a storm has brought down a large tree across a vulnerable length of raised boardwalk. Winter storms also sometimes create minor barricades of beach logs.

1. The trail begins clearly enough at the sea end of the parking lot, but you may be a little disoriented by the road that almost immediately cuts across it. This comparatively new road leads to a First Nation reserve. Cross it to find the real trailhead, indicated in part with a distance indicator of "1.02 km" (recently defaced).

2. From here to the beach it is virtually impossible to stray from the route, since it is almost entirely on boardwalk. Even more than on similar trails in the area, you will pass many strikingly "suspended" hemlocks: trees

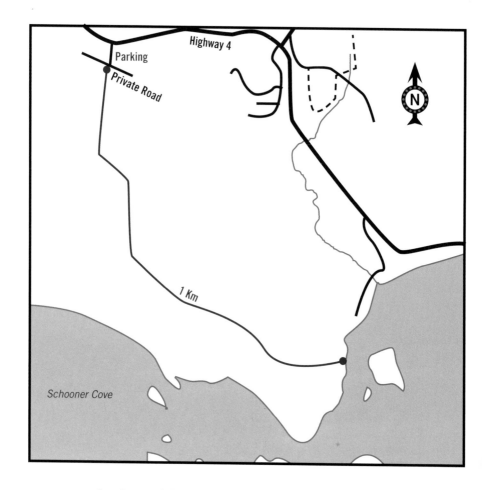

that began life as seedlings on rotting "nurse logs" but found themselves increasingly dependent on their own exposed roots to keep them upright as their original rootbase decayed away beneath them. On its way to the shore, the trail descends and ascends small ravines created by streams. The last section descends consistently to end at sea level. Take time en route to pose beside the heavily buttressed spruce with the specially constructed viewing platform.

3. Once on the shore you can walk many kilometres in either direction, though this may not be apparent at

first. You will immediately see that it is possible to hike the whole length of beach to your left. You can arrange a pickup at Incinerator Rock, Green Point or even Wickaninnish 15 km away. No such one-way arrangements are possible if you go the other direction, to your right. Generally, however, you will find almost complete solitude by heading that way. A warning, though: while you may find it easy to walk on the sand around the small rocky headland immediately along the beach, higher tides can require a bit of sure-footed scrambling to get over it or wading to get around it.

LEFT *A particularly large spruce near the shore. Tolerant to salt spray, spruce are often the dominant species along the shoreline. (2)*

BELOW *Incinerator Rock and Green Point are the only interruptions of the beach. (3)*

33. RADAR HILL BEACHES

A challenging trail through amazingly formed trees to small, isolated, sandy beaches facing the open ocean.

2 km return (plus beach-walking)	Difficult
Starting elevation and high point: 97 m	All seasons, but can be very wet

Start: At the T-junction where Highway 4 meets the road to Ucluelet, stop at the Pacific Rim Park visitor centre to buy a day parking pass. Turn right to stay on Highway 4 toward Tofino. After 22 km, turn left at the sign for Radar Hill. After 1.4 km, park in the paved lot closest to the seaward side of the hill.

Difficulty: This is a user-made trail, not part of the national park system of trails. It can be a wonderful adventure for those who like a challenge but daunting for those who are not sure-footed. A steep climb down roots followed by an extremely muddy track with many roots and logs requires some agility and balance. The wood can be slippery when wet. No matter how careful you are, you will get muddy feet, so don't wear good shoes. Wearing rubber boots will make crossing muddy sections comparatively easy, but the boots should be well-fitting and have good grip for climbing over logs.

1. The trail looks misleadingly easy and well used where it leaves the parking lot at the left-hand corner (viewed from the entrance to the parking lot).

2. In dry weather the increasing number of roots provide lots of steps and handholds to deal with the steepening decline. Before long you will come to the steepest section, a maze of intersecting roots. There is a rope here

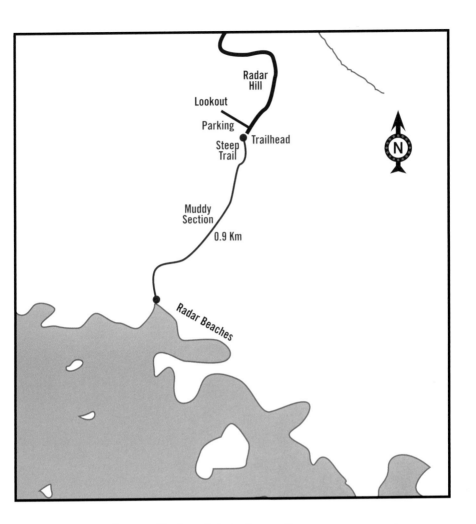

to grab, as well, though it isn't usually necessary except perhaps in very slippery conditions.

3. After descending about 70 m, the trail begins the second, muddy section. Be prepared to climb over deadfall. The mire is usually ankle-deep in the middle of the muddiest parts, but this will vary with the amount of recent rain and foot traffic. If you see small detour paths around muddy sections, you will generally find these are easier than the main route. Take time to pause and notice the fantastical formations of roots and twisted tree trunks,

mostly heavy with moss. Deer ferns, skunk cabbage and bunchberries are among the most attractive of the rich flora.

4. In the second part of the trail you will have to cross a small, slow stream a few times, but usually this is no more difficult than the muddy sections. When you see fish floats hanging from tree branches, don't assume you are nearing the shore. These are fun to see but not intended to indicate either the route (which is generally unmistakable) or your proximity to the shore, since the first one appears less than halfway along the route. You will probably hear surf when you are still a good distance from the end of the route, but when the trail becomes firm and dry you will know you are near the end.

5. The trail emerges into a large fan-shaped area of dune sand. Cross this to reach the beach. The easiest section to walk is to the right of the trailhead. If, however, you want to explore the maximum amount of coastline and are willing to clamber over some rocks and headlands, head left.

6. Return the way you came.

OPTION

When you return to your car, walk northwest along the paved walkway to the viewpoint with magnificent hilltop panoramas toward Tofino and Clayoquot Sound.

OPPOSITE TOP *Although quite steep and fairly slow, the first part of the trail is safe and not difficult for the nimble. (2)*

OPPOSITE BOTTOM *The north end of Radar Beach allows easy walking along firmly packed sand. Gowlland Rocks give a little protection from the full force of the waves. (6)*

34. TRENT RIVER ESTUARY

A loop route through estuary grasslands along a pebbly shore. Good views across Courtenay harbour. Expect to see lots of waterfowl, including great blue herons.

1.25-km loop	Easy
Elevation throughout: sea level	All seasons

Start: Some 11 km south of Courtenay, in the southern outskirts of Royston and just north of a small bridge over the Trent River, Carey Place leaves Highway 19A, the Island Highway South. Park at the end of the road between houses. You will see signs warning against collecting shellfish and asking you to restrain your dog.

Difficulty: Suitable for virtually everyone except those with severe walking difficulties. To allow the complete circular route, avoid high tides, since there is one section that can be wet at very high water. The vegetation can sometimes encroach on the path, so also avoid coming after a heavy dew or rain.

1. Your path begins with crossing a small, rocky dip that can be covered with water at very high tide, mostly in winter.

2. After a little easy walking, you will see a side track to the right. It is only a few metres down this path to the Trent River, if you wish to stroll along its banks a little.

3. Beyond the branch, keep going straight ahead to the shore. In mid-spring the track can be a little overgrown. A major feature of the trail is the richly coloured vegetation, particularly in late summer. As you get closer to the water, sea grass dominates the vegetation.

The trailhead on the shore looks toward Cape Lazo beyond Comox. (3)

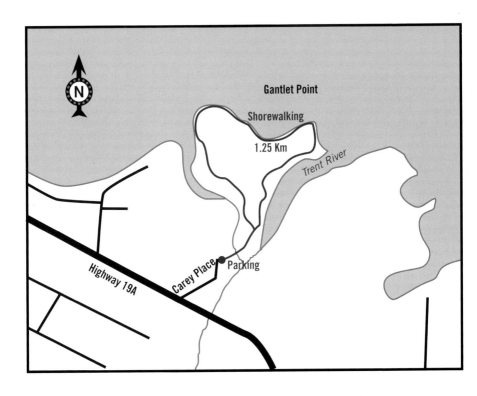

4. When you reach the pebbly shore, you can choose to pause for a picnic or scan the shallows for shorebirds, including great blue herons. Across Comox Harbour you will see the unusually shaped Goose Spit, site of both a military base and a provincial park. This stretch of shore comes to an end at Cape Lazo. Close by and to the south is Sandy Island Marine Provincial Park (a.k.a. "Tree Island"), which at low tide is connected to the much larger Denman Island. Turn left and follow the pebbly upper beach until you get to a former streambed. Thick growths of intertidal vegetation cover the lower beach.

5. To complete the loop, turn left and follow the edge of the streambed back to join your outbound trail and then your vehicle. At one point you may have to improvise the trail a little, since it fades and picks up again after a shallow dip.

35. SEAL BAY

Banktop forest trails, ravines rich with ferns, and a walk along pebbly upper shore. Lots of wildlife and shorebirds.

3.3-km loop	Easy to moderate
Starting elevation and high point: 52 m	All seasons

Start: At the main highway intersection at the north end of Courtenay, turn onto Ryan Road (you will see signs for the ferry and the airport) and drive 4.7 km to Anderton Road. Turn left and continue 3.8 km. The through road changes name to Waveland Road. Turn left onto Bates Road, signposted for Seal Bay, drive 1.6 km and park in the large signposted lot on the right. There are other trailheads on nearby roads, but the route described here begins at this one.

Difficulty: Most of the trails are broad and evenly surfaced with crushed gravel. The bank is quite high, though, requiring some exertion for those who aren't in particularly good shape, and the section along the shore involves walking on loose gravel and pebbles, as well as crossing some potentially slippery logs. Extremely high tides cover all but the narrowest strip of shore, requiring ducking under leaning trees and branches. Such tides are rare in summer (except some evenings) and can be avoided in winter.

1. Walking past the outhouses, go straight ahead and bear left onto the second trail toward the main beach. The forest here is second growth but mature and spaced enough to be attractive. Lots of undergrowth, primarily salal, adds to the settled feeling.

2. When you come to the "main beach trail," or "Don Apps Trail," avoid the temptation to descend the inviting switchbacks down the ravine. Carry on along the path parallel with the banktop.

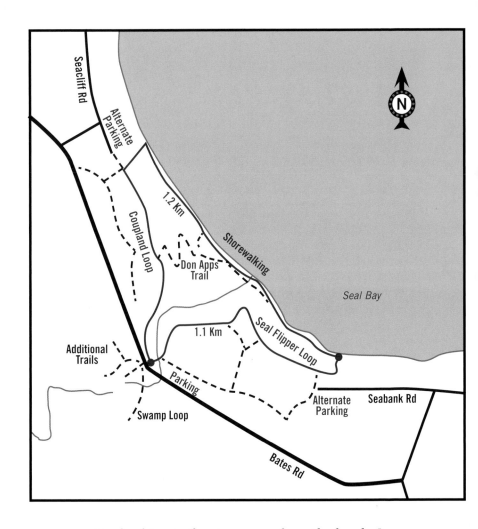

3. The banktop trail swings away from the beach. Ignore two options on your left, the first completing the Coupland Loop, the second leading past an alternative park entrance (off Seacliff Road).

4. Descend to the shore via the smoothly sloping trail and a set of concrete steps. Take care if wet logs have washed across the base of the stairs. Turn right along the shore for a little over a kilometre. Halfway along you will come to the end of the central trail to the beach (and an

ABOVE *Cormorants are common on this large offshore rock.* (4)

BELOW *The view southeast along the shore. At low tide a large sandbar is exposed, making for great barefoot walking.* (4)

outhouse). Keep your eyes open for wildlife, especially cormorants on a huge boulder a little offshore. When you come to a stream, particularly if it is full, turn up onto a shoreside trail and cross a small bridge before returning to the beach.

5. A short distance past a sign warning that the trail is closed you will find a new trail enabling you to climb back up to the bank to rejoin the upper trails. Once you have reached the top of the bank, turn right onto Seal Flipper Loop. Ignore the trail to the left partway along (though there is yet another outhouse a few metres down this path) and carry on to the ravine-top viewpoint with guardrails. Swing left to carry on along Seal Flipper Loop and follow the ravine back to your vehicle.

OPTIONS

If you still have lots of energy left and would like to explore the park further, you can walk for many more kilometres on other trails, all of them away from the seashore on the opposite side of Bates Road from the main parking lot. Easiest to follow is the horse/bike/jogging loop or the shorter Swamp Loop. You can usually find a paper map in a small wooden box by the main parking lot. The trails are well signposted.

The recommended trail to the shore descends along the side of a ravine thick with sword ferns. (4)

36. OYSTER RIVER NATURE PARK AND SALMON POINT

Known locally as the "pub-to-pub" walk. Begins with a network of trails through a forested park near a small river before arriving at the ocean. A sequence of winding trails, mostly near gravelly shore piled high with beach logs and giving magnificent mountain views.

6 km return	Easy
Elevation throughout: near sea level	All seasons

Start: At 22 km south of Campbell River on Highway 19A, and just north of the Oyster River Bridge, turn toward the ocean onto Glenmore Road and follow it to the T-junction with Regent Road. Some prefer to park a short distance to the right down Regent Road, in the Fishermen's Lodge parking lot, in order to make this a true pub-to-pub walk. However, parking at the Oyster River Community Park allows for more interesting forested trails through the small park.

Difficulty: The trails are all easy and have bridges over spots that are potentially wet if the river is high. Optional routes along the shore require care if the logs are wet and therefore slippery.

1. From the community park parking area, take the right fork of branching trails. This Fisherman's Trail, as the name suggests, angles toward the Oyster River. Unusual and interesting hemlocks line the generally flat path.

2. When you come to a convergence of trails with a utility hut, you will catch glimpses of the river down the short right branch. Carry on straight ahead to angle toward the river, and keep to the trail just back from the low bank. In spring

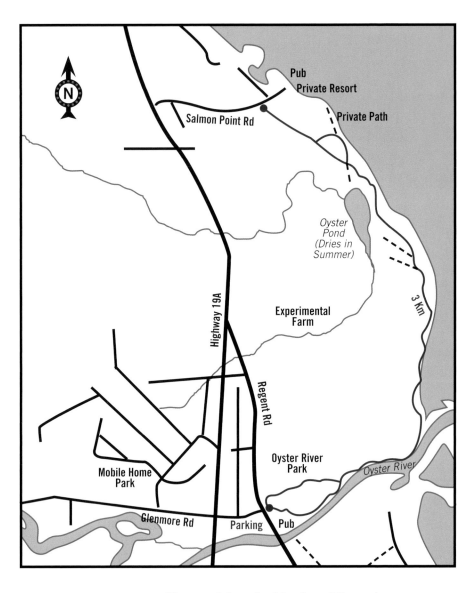

you can see trilliums, pink and white fawn lilies, salmon berry blossoms and bleeding hearts, as well as some huge black cottonwoods. Part of the riverside trail was closed as of spring 2013, but with an obvious detour and signs indicating the closure to be temporary. The trail crosses a new bridge over an old river channel and soon passes a sign saying "Padre's Walk." Shortly after this point, you can keep on through the trees for the short distance to the end of the park or dip down to the riverbank. If you walk along the riverbank, you may have to climb over a few logs, depending on the previous winter's storms.

3. The shoreline route, called Jack Hames Trail, changes character a little at various points, though the through trail is generally clear. After a section along a fence, then along an open meadow, the track dips down to run amongst beach logs. At points you will be between hedge-like vegetation, parallel to a fence outside large fields, or crossing a clearing dotted with small firs.

4. As you approach a wooded knoll, you will come to a spot where the trail splits, but several small detours all rejoin the main route. Side trails to the left lead to a small pond (Oyster Pond), great for observing water birds when full but subject to considerable drying over the summer. After passing the knoll, keep along the shore. Ignore the broad inland trail angling off to the left.

5. Near the end of the shoreline path, you will be stopped from further progress by a sign announcing that the track is to be used only by guests of a resort (clearly visible straight ahead). Take the considerably narrower path angling away from the shore through an open meadow. The going here can be wet during winter and early spring.

6. Reaching a convergence of trails, turn right onto a broad path, looking almost like a cobbled roadbed, through an area of low bushes. You will soon reach the end of the line at Salmon Point Road. From here you can turn right a short distance to the shorefront pub (to the left of the resort).

7. The return route is mostly the same as the outbound one. You can vary your track a little by going straight

ahead rather than heading left out to the shore at the first fork. This will take you toward the treed knoll, the pond and some short branch trails until you rejoin the shore trail for the return.

8. When you get back to the community park, you can take various ways back to your vehicle. Instead of crossing the little bridge, keep right to follow the track by the fence. At a fork, Ridge Trail to the left runs along the former riverbank, well above the flood plain. The right fork, Ferguson's Trail, leads straight back to the car park (though two smaller trails cross it). Ferguson's Trail is particularly distinctive for the interesting nurse logs supporting hemlock.

OPPOSITE TOP *The "crossroads" in the grassy meadow area near the northwest end of the trail by Salmon Point. (8)*

OPPOSITE BOTTOM *A bridge over a small tributary off the Oyster River in the Oyster River Nature Park. (2)*

BELOW *The mouth of the Oyster River. The trail runs through scattered trees immediately above the shore, but many prefer to walk along the shore parallel to the trail. (2)*

37. OYSTER BAY SHORELINE PROTECTION PARK

Sea meadows, broad sandy beach, historic breakwater, mountain views. Lots of shorebirds, eagles, seals. In the 1930s a relief camp and protected log boom area, now the site of a bird enhancement program for purple martins.

2 km (plus shorewalking)	Easy
Elevation throughout: sea level	All seasons

Start: At 20 km south of Campbell River and 27 km north of Courtenay on Highway 19A. Although you can park in the large paved lot indicated by the sign saying "Oyster Bay Shoreline Park," you will find the most satisfying loop walk starts at an unpaved spot at the southeast end of this area, by the "Rest Stop" sign.

Difficulty: In wet weather, logs can be slippery. Footing can also be unstable in loose sand. Otherwise, this is an extremely easy, safe route.

1. From the southeast end of the triangular-shaped area of sea meadows and small firs, walk along the upper beach to your left. Although you can walk through the parking and picnic area (complete with outhouses), the pleasantest hiking is along the edge of the shore, thick with beach logs.

2. After passing the parking lot, cut upward to the meadows onto the broad, level, crushed gravel trail leading through the centre of an open area and toward the base of the curving breakwater and spit. A user-made trail

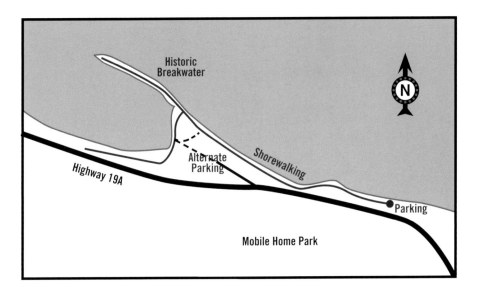

winds through the trees between the parking lot and the shore. You should, however, remain on established trails to protect the meadows.

3. Although a former breakwater here has been eroded to an uneven rocky ridge tapering to a gravel spit, it can be easily hiked. The tide will have to be out to allow walking to the end.

4. Returning to the grassy area, make your way along the broad path running by the protected bay with the pilings and birdhouses. The shore itself here doesn't make for good walking. As you get closer to the highway, at a spot where two paths cross, turn right to walk along the well-maintained path through the narrowing park (250 m).

5. When you reach the end of the park, return to your vehicle by any of the obvious routes.

OPTIONS

You can walk northwest along the shore below the highway for just about as long as you like. After 1 km, the highway swings away from the shoreline, so you will be walking in comparative quiet and isolation.

You can also go southeast along the shoreline, though it becomes rocky. After 1.5 km, your progress will be halted by the Salmon Point marina. (There is also a restaurant and pub there, as well as the beginning of a set of routes described in Walk 36, Salmon Point.)

BELOW *The trail toward the northwest end of the park. (4)*

OPPOSITE *The view directly across from the beginning of the walk encompasses many of the Coast Mountains' most spectacular peaks. At low tide the beach is at its most attractive, with hectares of fine sand and tidal pools. (1)*

38. BLINKHORN TRAIL

Telegraph Cove

A new, volunteer-made trail rising through forest past a few old-growth giants to a spectacular high viewpoint over the Broughton Islands before dropping to little "Stone Beach." The trail winds through a hemlock forest to a peninsula and a rocky little bluff lookout perfectly situated for spotting the famous orca pods that are common in the area.

7.8 km return (feels longer)	Moderate
Starting elevation: 10 m High point: 110 m	All seasons (high rainfall in winter)

Start: From Campbell River, drive 185 km north and west on Highway 19 toward Port Hardy. Turn off onto Beaver Cove Road, signposted for Telegraph Cove. After 10.5 km, turn left onto Telegraph Cove Road for 3.6 km. When you reach the tiny cove with its services, turn right onto Wastell Road following the signs to Telegraph Cove Resort campground. Drive through the campground, passing the signposted trailhead by site #98 and park in the trail parking spot by site #78. Obtain a parking pass from the campground manager or, failing that, from the Telegraph Cove office. (Some fascinatingly detailed information about the trail is available from the office, too, including the fact that the return trip requires 15,950 steps!)

Difficulty: This volunteer-made trail, "the property of no one" as a sign tells you, is carefully planned and signposted with more trail markers (blue and yellow) than you can find on any other route on the Island. You will cross many small bridges, most of them solid and easy, but one or two of the log bridges can be slippery (especially one with a yellow rope handrail). At a few spots the generally rooty path is quite steep, but ropes are in place to give a little security.

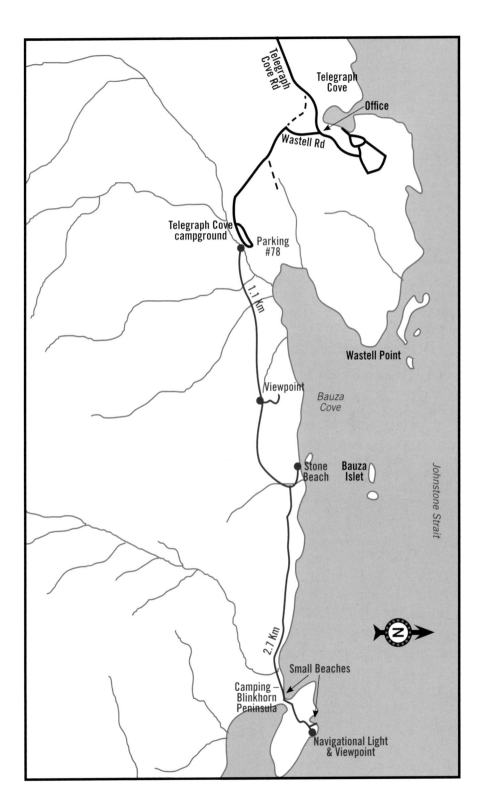

1. The trail traverses mostly uphill through largely second-growth hemlock but with a few old-growth giants. Near a clear-cut you will see an optional side trail to a culturally modified tree. After a sequence of rising crests, the trail levels off. You will find yourself in a deep cleft with a little outhouse labelled "bus stop" and an optional viewpoint trail to the left.

2. Climbing up and over the steep little ridge toward the viewpoint brings you down to one of the three chief beauty spots of the trail. The view over Wastell Point and Broughton Strait to the Broughton Islands is astounding.

3. After the viewpoint, the main trail begins to descend toward sea level, gradually at first, then over some increasingly steep sections. The route crosses a small stream from right to left and comes to a T-junction and a sign for a side trail to "Stone Beach." This 100-m path, flagged with red tape, brings you to a pretty spot with a jagged little beach and coastal views.

4. The trail next rises, unevenly, to run along the base of some cliffs through a fairly mature hemlock forest and a particularly gigantic cedar snag. Note the sign to a huge eagle nest and occasional traces of the historical telegraph line. From here the trail tends downhill to run fairly close to the shore, which is often visible through the trees. When you see Blinkhorn Peninsula jutting out toward you, you know you are nearing your destination. Soon the trail ends in a level camping area beside a gravel beach. As you will see, the "peninsula" is actually a forested island running parallel to the shore but connected to it by a narrow, gravelly isthmus.

5. Cross over the isthmus and angle up and over the island through some large fir, spruce and hemlock. Be aware that the isthmus becomes covered by the highest tides

(in summer only in the evening). As the trail drops toward the outer shore you will see an outhouse and one path leading toward a small rocky beach facing northwest. The right fork leads to a navigational light and a perfect spot for viewing the orcas that these waters are famous for. You are almost certain to find yourself in the company of kayakers also on the prowl for orcas.

6. Return by the same route.

ABOVE *"Stone Beach" is the first ocean access spot along the trail. (3)*

LEFT *This log bridge, over a small ravine, is provided with a securing hand cable. (4)*

39. SAN JOSEF BAY

Cape Scott Provincial Park

Easy trail through the best of West Coast flora, including a bog with miniature "umbrella" trees, deer ferns, saxifrage, bunchberries and some fantastically twisted, old-growth spruce and hemlock. Ends at a largely protected, perfect, white-sand beach with islets, sea caves and sea stacks. For many, it is a long way to drive for a single beach, but many would claim this to be the most beautiful one on the Island.

5.2 km return (plus beachwalking)	Easy (with moderately difficult option)
Elevation throughout: sea level	All seasons

Start: Just before Port Hardy, the northern terminus of Highway 19, turn onto the road signposted for Holberg and Cape Scott Provincial Park. The trip runs 64 km along almost entirely gravel roads. Make sure you have a full tank of fuel. (Gas is sometimes sold in Holberg, a tiny collection of houses.) As far as Holberg the road is broad and reasonably well graded, though fairly narrow toward the trailhead. Drive with your headlights on, since visibility can be poor in the dust clouds created by other vehicles. Always yield to logging trucks. Ignore somewhat confusing signs to the left just before the trailhead, one to a forestry campsite, the other to a private campsite and launching ramp.

Difficulty: In spite of its remoteness, this is among the easiest seashore trails on the Island. Even child strollers with large wheels can be used on the broad, level, crushed-gravel surface. Note, however, that walking the whole length of the 1.5 km beach requires rounding a headland at low tide. If, by accident or planning, you need to use the trail over the headland, be prepared for a steep, muddy climb and descent over tangles of roots.

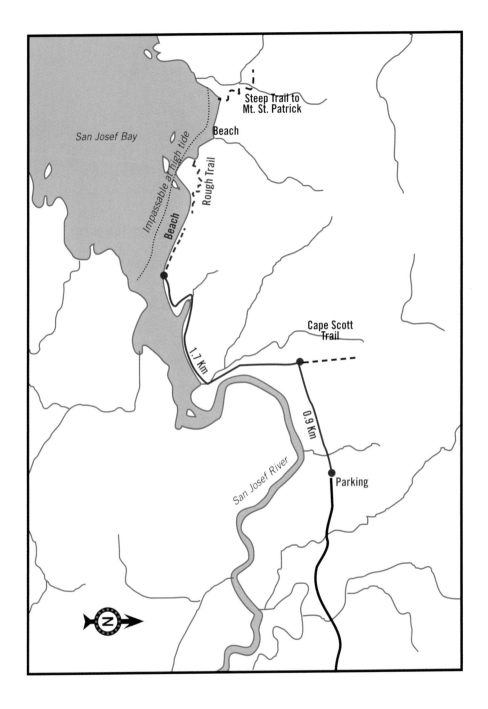

San Josef Bay

Steep Trail to
Mt. St. Patrick

Beach

Rough Trail

Impassable at high tide

Beach

1.7 Km

Cape Scott
Trail

0.9 Km

San Josef River

Parking

N

1. The first section of the trail is shared with backpackers heading for the multi-day trail to Cape Scott and possibly the North Coast Trail (a more difficult route requiring water transportation to its eastern end). The trail before this junction goes through light forest and, for part of it, slightly above a streambed.

2. At the junction with Cape Scott Trail, turn left toward signposted San Josef Bay. Part of this section passes through beautiful, coastal, bog vegetation. The pines and hemlocks, stunted by excessive wet, look like ornamental shrubs.

3. As you near the banks of the San Josef River the trail passes some amazing formations of old-growth spruce and hemlock. A bridge and a section of boardwalk enable you to cross a wet area easily. The trail arrives at the shore near the estuary. Here you will find outhouses and a bear cache for campers to store food. The trail continues along the upper shore, but most visitors prefer to walk along the 1.5-km beach. As noted earlier, be aware that you can pass the mid-beach headland only at low tide or via a steep and fairly difficult trail.

OPTION

The trail to Mt. St. Patrick at the north end of the beach is suitable only for those willing to face the challenge of climbing around and over slippery, twisted roots and through mud patches. Although the sign at the trailhead says the trail is dangerous, the only real hazard is that you might trip on a slippery root. The steepest part of the trail is immediately above the beach. Thereafter it drops to cross a stream and begins a gradual climb through generally small trees along the north side of the ridge. You will pass a few huge spruce toward the upper part of the trail and get glimpses of views to the north before reaching the largely open summit dotted with stunted trees. The trail is 5.6 km return and requires several hours. A more difficult trail branches off near the summit to head downhill to Sea Otter Cove to the north.

LEFT *A whole cluster of "sea stacks" and a sea cave at the north side of the headland*

BELOW *The islet can be explored only at low tide.*

URBAN PROMENADES AND BOARDWALKS

Most municipalities on Vancouver Island continue to develop waterfront walking opportunities. Needless to say, differing geographical issues and development priorities affect the final shape of the best efforts.

1. PORT HARDY

Start at the government dock and walk almost a kilometre along the seawall, first to Carrot Park, and make your way to Tsulquate Park. Features include chainsaw sculptures, a Japanese garden and good views of the harbour and the Coast Mountains. You can also start at Glen Lyon River and for more than 2 km follow the paved walkway along Hardy Bay. Cross an industrial park and the bridge at Highway 19, then pick up the Estuary Nature Trail along the head of the bay to Estuary Lookout.

2. CAMPBELL RIVER

The Rotary Seawalk runs 5.5 km between Highway 19A south of Campbell River and the shore. Start at the Marine Heritage Centre midtown or at the south end near Willow Point or at any spot between. Wheelchair accessible, the trail is paved the whole way. It passes through many small parks, some with washrooms and picnic tables. Frank James Park is distinctive for its many large wood carvings. For most of the way, the shore is easily accessible and great for paddling or picnicking on the sandy sections.

3. COURTENAY RIVER GREENWAY

Though it's called a "river" greenway, the southeast end runs along the shoreline of the harbour into which the river feeds. The promenade is probably most easily walked from the signposted access just off the old highway entering

Courtenay from the south. Running mostly behind houses and other buildings, it is well away from the rush of traffic. Low tide exposes a broad swath of fine sand in the outer harbour. The wide, even trail continues into Courtenay along the river and below the main shopping area to end at Lewis and Simms parks (though other routes connect from there for continued walking away from the sea).

4. QUALICUM BEACH

The concrete sidewalk along the edge of the seawall isn't continuous along the whole bay, but the interruptions are brief and easy to get past. Cafés and restaurants punctuate the 1-km route. Although the walk is separated from the highway only by a strip of lawn, the traffic is sedate. If you are willing to walk along the shore or on the sidewalk beside the road past a stretch of houses, you can extend the walk another 700 m to the Shady Rest Pub.

5. PARKSVILLE BOARDWALK

The easiest access is from the community park with its full facilities, several festivals and, for a number of weeks in summer, a famous sandcastle contest. The boardwalk itself runs along the upper shore between resorts on one side and the expansive, sandy, public beach on the other. At the southeast end the boardwalk links to a shoreside concrete walk leading to the end of the beach. The total length, one way, is just under 1 km.

6. NANAIMO HARBOURFRONT

Since the whole route is a little complex at its northwest end, many signs and maps are posted to guide you. There are many controversial plans to extend and simplify this part of the walk. Although this end requires passing around some businesses and parking lots, the walkway becomes increasingly natural and more consistently close to the water as it approaches Mill Stream. The section around Maffeo Sutton Park has many facilities and beautiful developments, including a tidal saltwater lagoon. The section below downtown Nanaimo passes next to marinas, shops and restaurants. Currently the route is 4 km long.

7. CROFTON BOARDWALK

Starting at the harbourfront, this impressive structure is raised on pilings for much of its route and punctuated with benches and access to wharfs. The second phase runs along the upper shore in front of an RV park. The third phase, recently completed, is a boardwalk leading all the way to Crofton Beach Park, a lovely little spot with a sandy beach and warm swimming water. The total walk is about 700 m each way.

8. BRENTWOOD BAY

A largely concrete walkway immediately above the shore runs more than 500 m along the most protected part of Brentwood Bay. The route is most easily approached from Marchant Road or Delamere Road (off Sea Drive). Houses and condos are above the route except where it crosses Ravine Park at the head of a narrow, little inlet. Views are mostly of the marinas with anchored boats and Daphne Island a little offshore.

9. PATRICIA BAY SCOTER TRAIL

Named after the little duck-like waterfowl that are common here, often in large flocks, the route runs next to the shore for more than a kilometre. Tsaykum Road, a fairly quiet residential street, is immediately above the trail for most of the route. The walk is probably best started at Patricia Bay Park off West Saanich Road, where park facilities are located. Since the bay is mostly mud flats at low tide, the views are probably prettiest at high tide.

10. SIDNEY "HEART SMART" WALK

Promoted by the local Rotary Club, this sequence of paved seawall walks starts slightly north of downtown Sidney and, after passing through small parks, runs next to Lochside Drive for a total of 2.5 km. It is probably most easily found by making your way to the end of Sidney's main road, Beacon Avenue. From here turn right to pass, in succession, Beacon Park, Eastview Park and Tulista Park before leaving the downtown behind and walking along a grassy strip between a long residential street and a largely level gravel shore.

11. GREATER VICTORIA

Victoria makes great use of its convoluted and picturesque coastline. Three of its municipalities in particular provide many kilometres of seaside walking along promenades, esplanades and boardwalks. Some of these are only a hundred or so metres long. Others go several kilometres. The following are among the best longer walks.

11a. Oak Bay Esplanade

From Beach Drive, the road that parallels the coast for much of Oak Bay, turn off and park by Willows Park (by Dalhousie Road). This route, a little over 1 km long, begins by crossing the park to the beginning of Esplanade. The road – and its sidewalk – run along the seawall above the beautiful sandy beach of Oak Bay. At the end of the road, follow the signposted route up the bank and through the bushy area to join Scenic Drive, which loops around Cattle Point. The view is primarily of Harrow Strait and various islands, some close, some in the US.

11b. Dallas Road: Ross Bay to Ogden Point

One of the prime features of the city, this sequence of side-walks, seawall walks and grassy parks is on the "must see" list for every visitor. While many drive the distance, the 4 km is best enjoyed on foot. Ogden Point breakwater at the west end of the section is a distinctive walk in itself, particularly if the seas are high or scuba divers are exploring the depths. The walk from there to Holland Point Park is the least popular part of the route. From this waterfront park, the route past Beacon Hill Park to Clover Point Park is the most popular. The easternmost section, along Dallas Road, has a reputation for sensational events. If a rare storm is blowing from the east, the waves can throw spray (and logs) over the seawall. The cemetery across the road from the east end of the bay is famous for bloodcurdling stories of satanic rituals and the like. The views to the Strait of Juan de Fuca and Olympic Mountains are superb.

11c. Westsong Walkway / Westbay Walkway

Many different roads allow access to this sequence of esplanades and boardwalks. Unlike most other such walks in the Greater Victoria area, this one runs next to roads only in relatively short sections. The west end of the walk begins off Head Street a little north of Westbay Marina in Esquimalt. This end of the walk uses many sections of boardwalk, often over water and below rocky bluffs. It passes below Barnard Park and winds as a concrete esplanade along the convoluted shore past Rainbow Park and Lime Bay Park before passing large condominium complexes and ending at the Johnson Street bridge. The route is a little over 2.7 km one way. The whole walk gives fascinating views of the boat traffic into and out of Victoria's Inner Harbour.

CONTACT INFORMATION

BC PARKS

www.env.gov.bc.ca/bcparks

PACIFIC RIM NATIONAL PARK

2040 Pacific Rim Hwy
Ucluelet, BC V0R 3A0
tel: 250.726.3500
fax: 250.726.3520
www.pc.gc.ca/eng/pn-np/bc/pacificrim/index.aspx

FISHERIES & OCEANS CANADA

(for tides and shellfish closures)
148 Port Augusta St
Comox, BC V9M 3N6
250.339.2031
Communications Branch
200 – 401 Burrard St
Vancouver, BC V6C 3S4
tel: 604.666.0384
fax: 604.666.1847
www.dfo-mpo.gc.ca/index-eng.htm

CAPITAL REGIONAL DISTRICT PARKS

Parks & Environmental Services
490 Atkins Ave
Victoria, BC V9B 2Z8
tel: 250.478.3344
fax: 250.478.5416
www.crd.bc.ca/parks

COMOX VALLEY REGIONAL DISTRICT PARKS AND TRAILS

600 Comox Rd
Courtenay, BC V9N 3P6
tel: 250.334.6000
toll free: 1.800.331.6007
www.comoxvalleyrd.ca/EN/main/community/parks-trails.html

COWICHAN VALLEY REGIONAL DISTRICT

175 Ingram St
Duncan, BC V9L 1N8
250.746.2500
1.800.665.3955
www.cvrd.bc.ca

REGIONAL DISTRICT OF NANAIMO

Recreation & Parks Services
Oceanside Place
830 W Island Hwy
Parksville, BC V9P 2X4
tel: 250.248.3252
toll free within BC: 1.888.828.2069
fax: 250.248.3159
recparks@rdn.bc.ca
www.rdn.bc.ca

ACKNOWLEDGEMENTS

Thanks to the friends and family who accompanied me on these trails, offered their opinions and pointed out details: Eileen Dombrowski, Megan Dombrowski, Bill Thompson, Aldous Sperl, Arno Dirks and Jim and Penny Cavers.